Your
Guardian
Angel
and
You

Your Guardian Angel and You

Denny Sargent

WEISER BOOKS

Boston, MA/York Beach, ME

First published in 2004 by
Red Wheel/Weiser, LLC
York Beach, ME
With offices at:
368 Congress Street
Boston, MA 02210
www.redwheelweiser.com

Library of Congress Cataloging-in-Publication Data
    Sargent, Denny.
            Your guardian angel and you / Denny Sargent.
                p. cm.
            Includes bibliographical references.
            ISBN 1-57863-275-7
                1. Guides (Spiritualism) 2. Guardian angels. I. Title.
        BF1275.G85S27 2004
        202'.15--dc22
                        2003019492

Typeset in Centaur by Garrett Brown

Printed in the United States
RRD

11 10 09 08 07 06 05 04
8 7 6 5 4 3 2 1

The paper used in this publication meets the minimum requirements of the American National Standard
for Information Sciences Permanence of Paper for Printed Library Materials Z39.48-1992 (R1997).

Holy Secret Centered Self
Blazing Sun in the distance
Shining unto me.
I pull thee from the starry womb
From the milk of Hathor's breast
To come, devour me!
Greatest glory of the angels
Unborn rune of God's creation
Fly thee hither as a dart
A bolt of fire
Of desire
And screaming, come to me!
Dissolve me in the putrefaction
Rend all matter from my breast
Then bury me in vessel lead.
Soon the ashes are igniting
And the dross has dropped away
Angel golden, all afire
Grasp me in thy sun-lit pyre
O desire, O desire!
Let two be none again!

—Aion (D. Sargent) 1978

CONTENTS

INTRODUCTION

Why are we on this planet? Is there a purpose or plan to our lives? Will God help you understand this plan and your place in it? Guardian Angels are God's most direct and personal answer to these questions. Your Guardian Angel exists to help you, explain to you, and guide you through the divine plan that you embody. If you follow the path that God has provided for you, you will find real happiness, real peace, and real freedom. These are the universal goals of life.

The key is to find your true will, the plan that God has provided for you, and follow it. Your whole life, really, is simply a search for what it is you are supposed to do in this life, and then do it to the best of your ability! But where do you start? By forming a solid and real connection with your Guardian Angel.

The goal of this book, first and foremost, is to simply tell you this: You can make an internal connection to a spiritual being who exists solely to help you find your way, your path, your plan, your true will. This being is your personal, direct connection with God. It is, in fact, a spark of God. This being is patiently guiding you and helping you every day. This being loves you deeply, no matter what you do or who you are. It was born with you, and will never abandon you, and will help you transition into another life when you die. You can call upon this being for real help and guidance at any time. If you choose, you can form a relationship with this being that is stronger than any other bond, and you can have real conversation with this being and so know what your divine will is!

When my wife was a teenager, she had an encounter with her Guardian Angel that changed her life. She was about to go to a party with several friends on a rainy night in her hometown. One of her pals had his car and was going to give them all a ride across town. As they approached the car, a winged figure appeared before her with its arms thrust forward, palms up, as if to push her away. In shock, she stopped. "Don't go," the angel said. Then the image faded away.

Her friends turned and yelled at her to hurry up. They obviously had not seen what she had. Thinking her imagination was playing tricks on her, she started walking to the car, until she felt a force pushing her back. She told her friends to go on without her, unable to ignore this strange warning. A deep unexplained sadness filled her as she said good-bye to her friends. They were puzzled and urged her to join them, but finally left without her. Ten minutes later, they died in a terrible car wreck.

This story, and others like it, have fascinated me and pushed me, much as my wife was pushed, into studying and writing about my Guardian Angel. I have followed the winding path of my Guardian Angel for over eighteen years with surprising and rewarding results. I have sought the Guardian Angel within myself and out in the world, and as my knowledge expanded, I came to realize that guardian spirits are universal. One of the communications I have received from my angel is that the information I have gathered must be shared with others, and so I hope that this work forms a small addition to such stories and teachings of the world.

For as long as human beings have been recording their thoughts, dreams, and ideas on stone, wood, or paper, there have been accounts of Guardian Angels. Today a fantastic number of people believe in them in a number of very surprising places. Across many different religions, the accepted views of Guardian Angels are remarkably the same. Just as a being of light saved my wife, so too do these beings appear in many times and places to offer advice, help, and healing.

Most of the stories involving Guardian Angels show us examples of divine intervention at moments of danger. Today, this seems to make up the majority of the many angel experiences that people report. These stories of rescuing angels have appeared in books, magazines, and newspapers, as well as in movies and on TV. One cannot escape the idea that angels, and particularly Guardian Angels, are making their presence known more and more to a variety of average people. But do we have to wait quietly until our lives are in danger before we can meet our Guardian Angels? The answer is no, and that is the reason for this book.

This book is a user's manual, not a book of feel-good philosophy or a collection of inspirational religious stories—although there are some good tales scattered here and there! This book has one purpose: to offer you simple non-mumbo-jumbo tools and techniques that will allow you to connect with, converse with, meet, and merge with your Guardian Angel.

This is not a fantasy, nor is it something only a few "chosen ones" can do. Anyone, and that means *you*, can meet and gain daily inspiration and guidance from your Guardian Angel. Although the process is actually fairly simple, it takes effort, courage, and determination. Most of all, it takes willpower. I know dozens of people who have made this journey or who are in the process, and they are just normal people like you and me. The difference is that they stumbled upon the keys to connecting and joining with their Guardian Angels just as I did. This book is my effort to demystify this hidden process and offer it to you on a silver platter.

Since you are holding this book in your hand, you have taken the first crucial step: You are curious and interested. Now you must take the next steps. Be aware that, just as with any relationship, your connection with your Guardian Angel can be as close as you want it to be. You can keep your relationship distant or you can literally begin the process of merging with your angel. The choice is up to you, as are all real choices.

Most traditions that acknowledge the presence and power of a Guardian Angel or Spirit agree on this: Making contact with this divine being requires some effort on your part. Your Guardian Angel opens doors and tries to help, but you must make an effort as well. Direct knowledge of or communication with your Guardian Angel requires work. Once the connection is made, a dialogue can be established and you can help yourself along the spiritual path. Many different religions believe that we fall into sin and error when we don't follow divine guidance. This can mean following particular rules or doctrines set down by traditions, but the real goal is to follow the will of God (or however you view the divine). Books or dogma cannot provide the kind of direct divine guidance that your Guardian Angel can offer on a day-to-day basis.

This book will give you the tools to make that effort. Part 1 contains a short history of the Guardian Angel as it has evolved through time in many different cultures. This will give you background and perspective that will help as you prepare to contact your Guardian Angel. It also outlines the process of in-depth self-exploration that is vital if you wish to become closer to your Guardian Angel.

Part 2 offers exercises and techniques that carry your relationship and your direct communication with your angel to new levels. It also explores ways to balance the new energies and changes that result directly from your deepened connection with your angel, and shows you how to ask questions of your Guardian Angel and get real answers. In this section, you'll also get to know your Shadow, the dark side of you that must be balanced and overruled by your Guardian Angel, and you'll learn ways that your angel can protect you spiritually.

Part 3 is, in a sense, the core or "inner mystery" of this book. It presents the key ritual or operation that, in ancient books of mysticism, is called "The Knowledge and Conversation of the Holy Guardian Angel." It gives step-by-step details of a ritual that is over 2000 years old—a process by which you can meet your Guardian Angel. It also reveals techniques and exercises for further uniting and merging directly with your Guardian Angel.

In the Appendices, you will find background on the universal appearance of the Guardian Angel or Guardian Spirit in a variety of spiritual traditions.

Please note that you can follow all or part of this process. You need not go through each and every step. Many people I have taught in seminars and workshops have been content simply to connect with their Guardian Angels, as described in the exercises in Part 1. Others want to go further with the process, using the exercises and techniques described in Part 2. Very few people that I know have actually gone through the whole intensive process as set out in Part 3. The choice is completely yours. Go as far as your will allows. You may even return to the process at a later date and take it further.

I truly believe that God has a plan for each of us. In this book, I use the term *True Will* for this plan. Each of us has things we are on this planet to learn and to do. You and your Guardian Angel—the emanation that God has given to you—are in this thing together. You can go as slowly or as fast as you wish in your personal dance of evolution and spiritual growth. It really is all up to you (*both* of you).

One thing I am sure of: All the things outlined in this book are real and practical and get results. I know, because I, along with many others, have done them with truly amazing success. In fact, this book exists *because* of my Guardian Angel. After I had taken myself through this process and chatted with many others who had done so, I began teaching workshops on it. I was curious to see if anyone could do this. I found out that, indeed, anyone can contact and communicate with their Guardian Angel. From that time on, my Guardian Angel began nagging me to share this information with the public. So here it is; now maybe I can get a little peace!

I am proud that Red Wheel/Weiser is publishing this book, and there is a very special reason why. The books I used to learn about the Guardian Angel and how to contact it were bought by me thirty years ago at a wonderful mystical bookstore in New York City. That store was called Weisers and was owned by the original Weiser Publishing company! Indeed, what goes around comes around and God very definitely has a sense of humor!

Now, a word about God. Got your attention, didn't I?

In this book, I use the term "God" quite frequently. I am fully aware that the term is used by billions of people around the world and that it means something different to just about everyone. I use it here because it is recognizable and a handy hook on which to hang a very big concept: the supreme life force that pervades and, indeed, *is* the universe. Possibly terms like OM or Tao or Goddess or Deity or Great Spirit may be more comfortable for you. When I use the term "God," I include all of these concepts and more in its meaning.

I do not believe in only one religion; I believe in universal truth. No one is excluded. God is love, in my humble opinion. There are no wrong ways to worship the divine if you do it with love and True Will, regardless of what religion, sect, or creed you profess. If you have reservations about my use of the term "God," please keep in mind the spirit in which I use it.

Likewise, the term "Guardian Angel" may be strange for some of you. No problem. Feel free to substitute the term "Guardian Spirit" if you prefer, or "Atman" or "Self" or any other term that means the same thing to you. The reality of the Guardian Angel is what is important, and it is as real as these words you are reading now. Terms come and go, your Guardian Angel is forever.

Now, it is time for you to meet the best friend, the wisest teacher, the closest mentor, and the coolest coach you have ever had: I'm proud to introduce you to your Guardian Angel!

Part I:

Meeting Your Guardian Angel

Chapter 1:

A Brief History of the Holy Guardian Angel

When you first meet people, you are usually curious about their identity and their intentions. What do they do? Where do they live and what are their hobbies? What kinds of friends and family do they have? In short, what is their history? You can't really begin to form a relationship with someone without first learning about his or her origins. The same thing applies to meeting and getting to know your Guardian Angel.

The word "angel" is quite old. It comes from the Sanskrit (the ancient tongue of India) word *angiras*, which means a "divine spirit." This term was carried by the sweep of nomadic invasions into Persia where it became the word for "courier" and finally entered Western culture as the Greek word *angelos*, which means "a messenger." This conforms to the traditional belief that angels are messengers of God. Angels are called "demigods" or "high spirits" in a wide range of cultures, both ancient and modern. Yet everywhere they are also seen as spiritual beings that bring messages from the divine world to man.

The idea of the Guardian Angel has permeated the folk beliefs of countless cultures. Some of the earliest writings we have from the Sumerians, the Egyptians, and the ancient Greeks indicate a strong belief in a personal deity. This "little god" was seen as a personal spirit or power that comes into the world when each person is born to help that person grow and prosper throughout life. According to these texts, this spirit is a part of you and yet it is somehow a higher being whose purpose is to watch over you, to guide you, and to help you in times of need.

It is remarkable how little this concept has changed, even within our Western culture. Virtually all ancient peoples believed in this concept and yet it is not a major part of any particular official doctrine. Instead it is something handed down within secret or mystery traditions. Many simply believe it without knowing why. Yet the certainty that we each have a Guardian Angel is widespread. If you ask people if they believe in Guardian Angels and why, a few will point to their religion, but most will simply say that they just feel that "a power" is watching over them.

Traditional Jewish mystics call angels "shining ones." They believe that each of us has a bit of God, an angel, assigned to protect us. The ramifications of this belief—

that a messenger, entity, or spirit that is born with you and watches over you through-out life—are many. For the ancients tell us there is a catch: You must make an effort to open up to your guardian spirit if you want direct help. It is a kind of divine part-nership. In ancient times, this was accepted. In our modern world, however, we don't address the issue of how to interface with this personal divine helper.

Older cultures provided worldviews filled with mystery, miracles, and the daily workings of the divine. A thousand years ago, a Saint who had visions was an accept-ed and respected figure. Omens and divine messages were the stock-in-trade of most folk cultures. In our haste to modernize under the banner of science, we seem to have gone too far in casting out all mystery and magic from our world. Our inner voices have been muffled and are often ignored.

After discussing the concept of a Guardian Angel with hundreds of people over many years, I have discovered many views of this being. I've spoken with Christians, Moslems, Jews, Buddhists, Pagans, and Animists, all of whom have remarkably similar yet divergent views of what a Guardian Angel is and does. The differences, in fact, seem to be merely facets of the same jewel—the Inner Self or Guardian Angel.

THE GUARDIAN ANGEL IN ANCIENT CULTURES

The word "religion" comes from the Latin term *religo*, meaning "to re-link." We tend to think of religions today as institutions, bureaucracies with a clear dogma or codi-fied set of beliefs that people accept. Yet hidden like a jewel within most religions sits this intriguing concept of the Guardian Angel.

From earliest times, ancient cultures have accepted that each person has a per-sonal deity or Guardian Angel. The ancient Greeks called this the "genius." This term has come down to us today to describe someone of great intelligence. After all, who could know more than your Guardian Angel? Ancient Egyptians referred to this being as the *Ka* and always showed it in carvings as a small being with the body of a bird and the head of a man. How like our traditional Western image of an angel this is! Egyptian texts claimed that the Ka departed from the body only at death. Pyramids and tombs often had a special exit passage for this purpose. The texts make it quite clear, however, that the Ka was not the soul, but rather a special divine being given to each person by the gods to protect the soul.

The Sumerians and other ancient cultures of the Middle East very likely influ-enced our concept of what an angel looks like. Temples and palaces were adorned with massive images of divine winged beings. The term for a guardian spirit in the ancient Chaldean tongue was *Il*, a "small god" born with each person to help and act as an inner divine protector throughout life. The term *Il* later evolved into the Hebrew term *El*, or God. It is interesting to note that even today, the term appears at the end of each angel's name, as a mark of the divine: Gabri-*el*, for example.

THE GUARDIAN ANGEL IN JUDAISM

Judaism retains a firm belief in Guardian Angels and is probably one of the main sources for angelic lore in both Christianity and Islam. Rabbinical doctrine states that there are angels assigned to each person, and that each nation and city has a Guardian Angel as well. In one place it even states that "every blade of grass has a Guardian Angel," a statement that reaches far into an animistic past when most believed that everything had a power or spirit dwelling in it.

Angels were extremely important in the birth and growth of Judaism and the Guardian Angel is still often ritually invoked to protect house and family. Although the belief has been almost lost within mainstream Judaism, it is still maintained within smaller orthodox groups.

THE GUARDIAN ANGEL IN CHRISTIANITY

The concept of the Guardian Angel, though not currently central to Christian doctrine, is still very present. Within the Roman Catholic Church there is a Guardian Angel Society. In Catholic schools, children are often taught to pray to their Guardian Angels and even to leave a section of their desks clear for their angels to rest upon! In the liturgical calendar of the Catholic Church, October 2 is set aside as the Feast of Archangels, a celebration that honors the Holy Guardian Angel. Numerous devotional images of the Guardian Angel have survived as well. One image that has seeped into popular culture can be found in shopping malls and catalogs as well as churches. This image depicts an androgynous being with long hair and huge wings uplifted, wearing shining robes, often with a star glowing above its head. The figure is often shown guiding children over a dangerous bridge or path. The message is clear: An angel has been sent by God to protect each of us, especially children.

Recently, interest in Guardian Angels has been revived within Catholicism and within Christianity as a whole. This is primarily a grassroots movement, although both the Pope and Billy Graham have responded to the renewed interest by publishing material on Guardian Angels! Those who seek Biblical proof of the Guardian Angel are pointed to Matthew 18:10 by believers. Here it is set forth that God has assigned a divine guardian to each of us, a fascinating concept that may be in the process of reinvigorating many Christian churches as people search for a personal link to the divine.

THE GUARDIAN ANGEL IN ISLAM

Islam is another religion that acknowledges Guardian Angels as direct connections with Allah (God), and as blessings sent by Allah to each of us to help guide us through life. Angels in general are quite common in the Koran. The Koran states: "He [God] sends forth guardians who watch over you and carry away your souls without fail when death overtakes you."

Angels appear throughout the Islamic holy book. Gabriel was the angel who gave the Koran to the prophet Mohammed. There are a number of other angels in Islam, like Ithurial, who helped make Adam and who will preside over the last judgment.

THE GUARDIAN ANGEL IN BUDDHISM AND HINDUISM

Many people are very surprised to find angels in Asian beliefs! Yet, there they are! In fact, the belief in an inner divine presence that guards and helps us is very common in Eastern religions. In Buddhism there are angelic protectors sent from heaven to protect and guard the faithful. Winged angels are often depicted in Buddhist art, especially on the ceilings of temples. They are shown lifting Buddha to heaven after he died.

Divine angels who cluster about Amitabha Buddha in heaven often are said to deliver inspiration and messages to people still living. Buddhist sects, in fact, teach a very interesting point—the idea that each person has within a seed called the *Budhi*. This light or energy is a direct connection with the universe and is one of the core tenets of Buddhism. Everyone is a potential Buddha. Everyone is on his/her way to attaining enlightenment. What is needed is a guide and the guide is this guardian spirit who is the real Self. These words are nearly identical to those used in other religions to describe Guardian Angels. The common Buddhist mantra or chant that shows this clearly is: *OM MANI PADME HUM*. This means: "The jewel (Higher Self) in the center of the lotus (body)"

Hinduism, as different as it is from Western religions, still carries the belief that every person has a Guardian Angel, or Atman. The Atman is often described as a Higher Self, or as a spark of God that guards and guides. Hinduism also teaches that every living thing has a *deva* or angel to make it grow or help it prosper. The goal of the practice of yoga and of devotion to or worship of many different forms of the one God is to attain this enlightenment. All religious Hindus work to gain complete understanding and union (yoga) with the universe, and it is the Atman (or Guardian Spirit) that urges us on toward this, leading us and showing us the way.

THE GUARDIAN ANGEL IN EARTH-CENTERED RELIGIONS

Other cultures that are more connected with the Earth and its natural cycles, such as Native Americans, aboriginal or tribal groups, Afro-Caribbean sects, and modern Pagans, tend to be Pantheistic and diverse. This means that their traditions are rooted in a belief that the divine is everywhere and has many aspects. In these varied faiths all things are seen as alive and everything has a spirit. Yet as different as these faiths are from traditional Western faiths, they virtually all acknowledge a Guardian Spirit.

The Guardian Spirit or Angel in these cultures is often called "the Ally" or "totem." It is remarkable how similar this concept is to that of the Guardian Angel of established religions. The teaching in such Pagan cultures (from *pagani*, people of the Earth) often reveals that, although each person has an Ally or Guardian Spirit, each must make an effort to connect with this spirit through some sort of initiation or "vision quest." Once the connection is made, this ally or totem will be a constant psychic companion and will always help advise, protect, and guard the individual. Sometimes this Guardian takes the form of a spirit animal. Once this bond is created, the Guardian can always be called upon in magical ceremonies and rituals to accomplish certain things. This initiation or quest, as we will see, is very much in line with the ritual we will explore later.

THE GUARDIAN ANGEL IN MODERN TIMES

Our modern culture is primarily a scientific and, in many ways, a psychological culture. There is a very strong basis for belief in a Guardian Angel in popular psychology, believe it or not! Most people believe they have a conscience, even if they've never thought carefully about it before. We believe that there is a kind of internal compass that indicates to us what is right and what is wrong.

Terms like "conscience" or "intuition" are simply modern names for the Guardian Angel. It is that little voice inside our heads that tells us what is right, that feeling you have when you know you are doing something that is not correct, or that hunch you have that something will or will not work out. These occurrences, several centuries ago, would have been called guidance from the Guardian Angel. The more things change, the more they stay the same!

The person who really brought psychology and religion together and managed to define a modern concept of the Guardian Angel was C. G. Jung. Jung believed that there is a spiritual dimension to the inner mind, and that not all psychological issues can be ascribed to repressed sexuality or childhood trauma, as Freud held. Jung spent most of his life exploring a kind of logical spirituality. His chief contribution to the search for the Guardian Angel is his concept of Self—with a capital "S".

Jung believed that each person undergoes a process of spiritual and psychological growth. He studied the art and poetry of his patients as they were healing and changing. Over years of such study he came up with a theory about spiritual and psychic growth that he called "individuation," a concept that neatly connects with the concept of a Guardian Angel. Individuation is the psychic evolution of a person's inner Self. As each person grows, as the conscious and unconscious mind interface, as experiences and ideas mature, what emerges from the inner mind is a stronger link with a personified higher consciousness that Jung termed the Self. It is this higher consciousness that guides and advises each person, acting as a separate divine entity. This awakened spirit of the inner mind is, simply put, the Guardian Angel.

For Jung, the goal of life and of spiritual growth was this process of individuation, this process of increasing communication with the Self. As a person grows spiritually, as individuation occurs, his or her Self becomes more conscious and eventually becomes more a part of the person's life. It is all a matter of perception: becoming aware of your self is the same as encountering and becoming closer to your Guardian Angel.

This modern view of the Guardian Angel is not really very different from the older religious view. In fact, they are two different views of the same thing. One of the great maxims of the ancient mystics was, "As above, so below." This has been filtered through the lens of modern psychology to become, "As without, so within," reflecting a belief that external reality mirrors internal reality. What is in heaven is also on the Earth; what is in the external world is also in the internal world. Both this modern view and the ancient religious concept of the Guardian Angel express the idea that with conscious effort you can contact and communicate with your Self, or your Guardian Angel, and reap fantastic benefits and good guidance.

Chapter 2:

Preparing to Meet
Your Guardian Angel

Encountering your Guardian Angel can change your life. This powerful relationship has reenergized people, added depth to friendships and marriages, encouraged people to leave abusive relationships, and helped alcoholics stay sober. It
has brought people to a deeper understanding of their faith and to more compassion-
ate and empathetic actions in their daily lives. It has, in every instance, helped people
discover their true wills, the actions that they should be taking on this Earth, and the
hidden talents they have within them that have gone undeveloped. However, before you
can make this connection with your angel, you must come to terms with ideas and
expectations concerning it.

Different accounts from different cultures portray angels as superhuman beings
with powers and abilities that can be called divine or supernatural. When angels appear,
they are always accompanied by amazing waves of pure love and power. They almost
always appear as beings of light. Sometimes they come as balls of light, sometimes as
glowing bands of light. When they appear in human form, they are often seen with
large sweeping wings and beautiful faces and bodies. Sometimes they are naked, but
more often they are clothed in flowing robes of light. White is the color most often
attributed to them, although many different colors are also mentioned in various historical accounts.

There are basically two types of angels explained in holy books and legends. The
Greater Angels, or Archangels like Gabriel who announced the birth of Jesus and is
said to have given the Koran to Mohammed, have great power. They are said to guide
the planets, the stars, and the course of cosmic events. Archangels guide the Jewish
tribes (Israel is an angel!) and guard the gates of Buddhist paradise. These Greater
Angels do the work of the ultimate power, or God. They appear at cosmic events and
as participants in the past creation and the future destruction of the world. These
Archangels, according to all the religions mentioned here, are beyond the reach of most
humans. They appear in the mundane world only when God sends them forth to act,
and it is unlikely that anyone reading this book will receive a divine visitation from one
of these great beings—although you never know!

It is Lesser Angels, also called Guardian Angels, with which we wish to concern
ourselves, however. In many traditions these angels are said to guard, protect, and guide

all living things. Although plants, animals, cities, and nations are also reported to have Guardian Angels, the most important are those assigned to human beings. When I refer to Guardian Angels, I mean the divine spirits who help and protect each of us from the moment of birth until the day we leave this Earth.

Guardian Angels, even in ancient texts, are described as divine beings assigned to each person at birth. They embody the will and true understanding of their charge and their job is to protect and help that person through the dangers and transitions of life. They represent, in essence, each person's direct connection to God. The function of the Guardian Angel is the same today as it has been throughout history.

Angels are different from us in important ways, however, and there is a tremendous gap between us. We can bridge this gap through love and will. Traditionally, your angel will make the loving effort to bridge this gap and reveal itself to you, usually at a time of extreme need. Yet there are many ways that you can expand your awareness and bridge the gap if you have the love and the will, and use the right techniques.

You have only very limited senses with which to perceive the world, so you can't normally see angels who may be around you. These beings are as real as you, but they are formed of a different kind of energy, an energy that is usually beyond your perception. You can see only a small part of the light spectrum. You can't, for example, see ultraviolet light, but you know it exists nonetheless. Anyone who has been around pets knows that people usually feel, smell, and hear only a fraction of what many animals can. I've seen fish jumping and birds screeching just before a minor earthquake, and it is obvious that most pets have a sense of smell that far surpasses ours. Though this may seem to indicate that we are limited creatures, it merely shows that most of us don't seek to enlarge the scope of our experience, of our senses. But we could see and hear more if we wanted to.

Just because you cannot immediately perceive something does not mean it is not real. Your mind "tunes out" many things around you all the time, but if you really pay attention, you'll be amazed by what you are missing. One of the keys to connecting with your angel is to increase your ability to perceive. If you are not listening for something, you won't hear it, but if you concentrate with real focus on your senses, it is remarkable what you will pick up. In this way, you can signal your angel that you are ready and willing to communicate, that you are reaching toward its higher level of perception and awareness. Your angel is waiting for such a signal.

Angels are beings of pure spirit and energy that have a higher level of consciousness. It therefore makes sense that your angel can be near you at all times without you sensing its presence in your day-to-day life. You have accepted your limited sense as the norm of your existence. But you can change your expectations so that you can bridge the gap between you and your angel. With effort you can sense and accomplish things that some would call miracles. Witness the stories of holy men and women around the world who have connected with the divine through love and dedication. The key is to expand your awareness, both of what is around you and what is within you. By using effective visualization techniques, meditations, mental exercises, and prayers, you can see and communicate with your Guardian Angel. Begin by preparing your mind, body, and spirit.

PREPARING TO COMMUNICATE WITH YOUR GUARDIAN ANGEL

Before you begin to communicate with your Guardian Angel, you must prepare yourself by opening your senses and your mind. It generally requires both mental and emotional preparation before you are ready to meet and form a lasting relationship with your angel.

Mental preparation is perhaps the most important task. Before you can deal with something or communicate with it, you have to accept that it exists. How many times have you walked past a new picture on the wall or a book out of place on a shelf and not seen it? You missed seeing it because your mind did not expect to see it! I often lose my keys. Sometimes they are right in front of me, but if they are out of place I often just don't "see" them until my wife points them out. She can see them because she doesn't expect them to be elsewhere, I can't see them because I don't expect to see them there.

What does this have to do with your angel? You need to realize that your angel can be next to you without you always being aware of it. All it takes is a simple shift in perception to reveal this divine being to you! It's not that your angel appears or disappears; it is simply that you change your viewpoint. The other day, I sat next to a friend on a bus without even noticing her. She didn't notice me either! After a few minutes, of course, we both recognized each other and laughed. We hadn't expected to see each other on that bus, and so we simply didn't. One minute she was just a nameless person; a second later, she "appeared" as my friend! In just this way, you don't expect to meet your Guardian Angel, so you don't. So, the first step in preparing yourself to meet your Guardian Angel is to change your expectations—change what you think you will experience. Cultivate a belief that your angel exists and that you will meet it if you simply shift your perceptions. When you do, you'll be halfway down the path to connecting with your Guardian Angel.

If you're not 100-percent positive that your Guardian Angel exists, try this simple exercise.

Exercise I: Touching Your Guardian Angel

Go to a park or a quiet place in the woods. Natural settings are usually best for this exercise, but a quiet room will work as well. Do this at a time when you will not be disturbed. It should be very quiet and peaceful and you should be feeling this way as well. If you are in pain or worried about something, wait until another time. Sit comfortably and close your eyes. Imagine a ring of white light around you and see all your problems and the nagging voices of others fading away until you hear nothing but silence. Then, without planning anything, call upon your angel to come to you, to reveal itself to you. Ask it to give you a sign of some kind so that you can begin the work of communicating with it. You'll probably say something like this, but please choose your own words:

Guardian Angel come to me
I love you and wish to know you
Touch me so I may understand you
Help me to grow and to prosper
Give me a sign, Guardian Angel
So that I may truly and deeply believe in you

You may want to repeat your small prayer several times, but the most important thing is to will this connection with love. After you have spoken, empty your mind completely of all thoughts and feelings and wait. After a period of about fifteen minutes (you decide), thank your angel and see the ring of white light enter your body and fill you with a calm feeling. See the light flow into the earth. Then leave and write down any thoughts, feelings, images, or sounds you experienced. If nothing happened, wait with an open mind. The sign you are waiting for may be subtle and it may not be what you expect. This is the second part of changing expectations: accepting communication without judging.

A friend who did this exercise was very disappointed when he did not receive a voice or image. He had been expecting a fantastic vision—flashing lights or something dramatic. He became very cynical until he got home. There was a magazine waiting for him in his mailbox. It had a picture of an angel on it and the headline, "Are Angels Real?" He knew then and there that his Guardian Angel was real, that this was the sign he'd asked for.

We are told that "the Lord moves in mysterious ways," and this is an important lesson to remember. Your Guardian Angel will contact you, of this there is no doubt, but will you be sharp enough or open enough to receive the contact? Only if you keep an open mind as to the form that this communication will take! By sharpening your sense and perceptions, you will develop a kind of sixth sense that will help you as you embark on this journey. Remember how limited your intellect is. It may not have been rational for my friend to see that angel magazine as a sign from his angel, but he knew, in his gut, that it was. To prepare yourself to communicate with your Guardian Angel, be open. Learn to really trust in your intuition.

It is equally important that you prepare yourself emotionally to contact your angel or you will have problems in your quest. Emotional preparation is really just another way of saying that you should be emotionally open and ready for the loving experience of meeting your angel, and that you should become more aware of the emotions you project. Certain emotions attract angels and facilitate communication, much as a lovely-smelling flower attracts a bee. Love, compassion, kindness, curiosity, and joy are all emotional states that seem to do this. Anger, jealousy, selfishness, cruelty, and guilt are emotional states that either repel angels or create barriers they cannot break through. Just as agitation muddies the water of a pond, making it impossible to see the bottom, negative emotional states muddy the mind so that the clarity necessary for dealing with the Guardian Angel is obliterated. Here is a very simple exercise for removing negative feelings and invoking peace, calm, and love.

Exercise 2: Cleansing Negative Emotional States

Find a tree in a quiet place, lean against it, and close your eyes. Feel the life of the tree. Feel the sap flowing in the trunk; feel the water and nutrients coming through the roots; feel the branches swaying and the leaves breathing. Breathe in deeply. When you breathe out, see your negative feelings leaving your body as a cloud of black smoke that flows into the tree, up the trunk, and out the leaves into the sky. As you breathe in, feel positive healing energy enter you from the roots, through the tree trunk, and then pervade you as a green light. Continue this process until you feel good. When you're done, thank the tree, thank your angel, and move on.

There is a lesson here that you should embrace if you really want to contact your Guardian Angel, a lesson learned by people who have had near-death experiences: Life is a miracle and filled with joy, if you but take the time and open your eyes to look. When I was fourteen, my breathing stopped for five minutes and my heart stopped for one minute due to a lung problem. When I was revived, my view of all things had changed subtly. I believe that this open, new appreciation for all things greatly helped me when, later in life, I set out to contact my angel.

When preparing to contact your Guardian Angel, you must also practice forgiveness. Ultimately, only God can judge. For your own health and progress, it is better to forgive those about whom you have bad feelings. Here is an excellent exercise for doing this and for emotionally "clearing the decks" before contacting your angel.

Exercise 3: Removing Obstacles from Your Path

In a quiet place, during a time when you will not be disturbed, sit down with a clean piece of paper and a pencil. Fold the paper into three sections. In one section, write "angry"; in another, write "jealous"; in another, write "afraid." In each section, write the things and the people that create these emotions for you. For example, when I did this I put my neighbor's name under "angry" because her dog is always barking and she won't deal with it. I put my friend's name under "jealous" because he makes more than twice the salary I do. I put terrorists under "fear" because, well, they frighten me! You should put down everything that triggers these emotions. When you are done, close your eyes and imagine a white circle of light around you and the paper. Read each list, saying as you do that you no longer feel that feeling. Then let the feeling go. For example, I said, "I am no longer angry with my neighbor, may my anger change to love. I am no longer jealous of my friend, I have all that I need. I no longer fear terrorists, they can not hurt my spirit."

It is very important that you feel the feeling as you say it, then repeat your statement over and over and feel the anger or fear or jealousy slowly dissolve in the white light surrounding you. It is really up to you to say what works to banish these negative thoughts. The important thing (and the hardest thing) is to acknowledge your negative feelings so you can let go of them.

Your angel wants to tell you and show you how to achieve real peace, real freedom, and real happiness. If you seem likely to use these things to better the world, you will motivate your Guardian Angel to bring them to you. Bitter, angry, and unhappy people do not care about such things, so they are signaling their angels not to come near. Angels never go where they are not wanted.

By choosing a positive response to the challenges of life and to negative assaults from others, you create a positive vibration that attracts your angel. Over and over, I have seen people who could not connect with their angels change their attitudes or let go of old negative emotions and—sure enough!—their angels were right there for them. Your Guardian Angel will never abandon you, never leave you, but that doesn't guarantee that you will see or communicate with it!

So, think positively! Seek the positive in every encounter and in every chore. Let go of negative emotions as soon as possible and forgive long-standing hurts. In this way, you will really prepare the way for your angel to embrace you. You will also be a happier, healthier person. Compassion is the key.

WHAT TO EXPECT FROM YOUR GUARDIAN ANGEL

Preparing to meet your Guardian Angel is like getting ready to meet someone of importance—a movie star or a long-lost famous relative. You may feel nervous, thrilled, and excited, and you want to get the relationship off on the right foot, but you may have a lingering fear that you will "blow it" or do something really dumb that will sabotage the whole encounter.

Don't worry! Accept the fact that your angel truly loves you and exists simply to help, guide, and protect you. It is so rare in life to meet someone who unconditionally loves and wants to help you that it is a difficult thing to completely accept. Most us, even if unconsciously, think that others act out of selfish motives. This is the way of the world, after all. But angels are very different beings. Since being wary of or ignoring your angel can hinder full communication with it, you must begin to visualize your angel as having several aspects.

Guardian Angels have several functions and so may appear slightly different to you depending on the task the angel is accomplishing at that time. For example, much as I am a teacher, a father, a sailor, and a writer (a few of my many "aspects"), your Guardian Angel may appear as a bodyguard, a healer, a dear friend, a counselor, a parent, or a guide. These are, of course, just a few of the hats that Guardian Angels can wear. By examining and pondering them, you can develop an attitude that will attract your angel.

Most stories you hear about people contacting their Guardian Angels refer to the angel as a bodyguard, a kind of divine rescuer. There are stories of accidents prevented by angels, lost and endangered children located by angels, and people warned by angels of dangerous situations. A man I met in a seminar recounted the strange feeling he once had that his inner voice was telling him not to take a particular commuter plane. He changed reservations and later found out that there was an accident with the plane on the runway. He will never forget that feeling of urgency that was almost a voice.

In just this way, your angel is even now guarding you, and the proof is buried in your memory, though you may not realize it. Think of all the times you suddenly decided to take a different road home or you made a change in travel plans. Maybe you had a hunch or heard an inner voice telling to do or not do something. This is how your angel helps protect you. Have you ever been convinced that you were about to be in an accident, but the car somehow missed you? Close your eyes, remember the last time you or someone you love miraculously avoided injury or an accident or was saved from a big mess. Remember this now. Did you feel an unseen hand? Did you say "thank God" or "someone must be watching out for me" or something like that? Accept the fact that your angel was present as a bodyguard.

Just as you may call for help when danger threatens, so you may call for healing when illness strikes. I was born with a birthmark on my stomach. Before I moved abroad, I had a checkup and the doctor, concerned, performed a biopsy that came back negative. Several years later, after returning to America, I kept getting a weird feeling that the birthmark was strange. My wife and others assured me that it had not changed and that I was mistaken. My angel kept pushing me in many ways to have it examined, so I arranged to see my doctor. The mark had become cancerous. It was easily removed and has given me no problems ever since. But if I had waited even a short time, the result might have been different.

There are many stories similar to mine. There are also many stories about angelic healings. Although Guardian Angels usually bring messages, they can also bring healing energy. Sophia had had chronic asthma since birth, sometimes serious enough to require hospitalization. After contacting and working with her angel for a year, her asthma gradually faded away. It is now rare for her to use the medication she once used a dozen times a day. Such cures are not uncommon.

Calling upon the divine for healing is a time-honored tradition in all religious faiths.

It is one thing to hope for divine healing, but if you actually expect and are listening for advice from your angel, you will often get it. With your eyes closed, think of all the times you or a loved one has been seriously ill and think about how that crisis was resolved. Did you ask for divine help? What did you feel? How were these health-crisis moments different from other times? When you asked for help, did you heal faster? Remember these times. Can't you see the sympathetic and loving presence of your angel beside you?

We unconsciously ask for help all the time, without even thinking about it. Your angel will often respond quickest to these heartfelt pleas. When my child is ill, I hold him and wish him better. Sometimes I sing or hum a song to him, visualizing him relaxing and getting well, seeing energy healing him. I feel this power and healing love most when I am drained and tired, but my child needs healing energy. It is then that I call upon my angel for strength. Suddenly, I feel it flow through me and I know its source. Guardian Angels are always attracted to this energy of need and will help, especially if the need is based on a selfless love. The angel is a healer, but it is your love and will that prompts the divine energy of healing to flow.

When you view your angel as your best, most beloved friend, you prepare yourself most effectively for contact and communication. The better you are at emotionally and mentally visualizing your angel, the easier it is for you to communicate with it. Remember that you have nothing to fear from a being who has nothing but love for you. Have you ever felt very depressed and lost? Have you ever been so full of pain from a loss or from a broken heart that you couldn't stand it? When you called out for help, did you get an answer? What form did it take? A call from a friend? A beautiful flower? The feeling of a hand on your shoulder? A gorgeous sunset? Now, close your eyes and remember such a time of emotional sorrow. Were you helped when you asked for it? Can you see your angel near you, comforting you? Your angel probably couldn't contact you because you were not ready to hear or see it, but that didn't stop your divine guardian from trying to help. When you make that connection, that contact with your angel, such comfort as it can give will be much easier for you to feel and understand.

When my grandmother died after a long and exciting life, I was deeply sad. I called to my angel for a little help and amazing things happened. Friends called long distance "by chance," letters from friends overseas appeared, and strangers seemed to go out of their way to be kind. None of these people knew about my loss, but all seemed to want to comfort me! When traveling I have often called to my angel for friendly help. Once, when I was stranded in a small town with no money and no place to stay, I called for a little friendly help and, suddenly, a car full of kids pulled up and asked me if I wanted to camp with them! It was a wild night, but you get what you ask for—whether or not it is what you expect! Angels, needless to say, can have a very funny sense of humor!

Guardian Angels can also act like parents, loving and yet sometimes stern. Have you ever seen a parent walking behind a small exploring toddler? The child often doesn't realize the parent is hovering nearby until he approaches something dangerous then, zip! The parent is right there with a guiding hand. You, like a child, often stumble and fall or reach out to touch something dangerous as you wander and explore your world. It is your angel's hand that guides you away from dangers and toward positive experiences. Unfortunately, like a willful but stubborn child, you may ignore or tune out your angel "parent." That's when you really get into trouble! But even as a parent will never abandon a wayward child, so your angel (probably sighing and shaking its head) will keep encouraging you to mend your ways and travel the right path.

Guardian Angels hate disharmony, anger, and grudges! Just like a kind parent, your angel may also can give you a spiritual scolding at times! How many times have you done something that wasn't so nice and suddenly—pow!—something strange happens? You yell at your friend and then you break a glass. You make fun of someone and suddenly fall down and find yourself being laughed at! Be aware that your Guardian Angel *is* real.

If you start with the idea that you live on this Earth to learn, to grow, and to heal others, then being pushed and prodded to make the correct decisions makes sense. It is, literally, in your best spiritual interest to be kind, loving, and helpful to all living things. "As ye sow, so shall ye reap" is not just a helpful saying; it describes the balance of the universe. It is said that a good deed returns to you a thousandfold; and so does a bad deed. Your Guardian Angel, like a loving parent, wants you to eat right, take care of your physical and emotional health, play well with others, and succeed in your life. Your joy at attaining your dreams is shared by your Guardian Angel, because, unlike you, it sees the "big picture"—the universal brotherhood, tolerance, and good will toward which all angels are working.

Guardian Angels are often most clearly revealed as personal guides into the unknown at the time of death. Many have reported seeing and talking to their Guardian Angels as they approach death. The message the angels give these people is always the same: Don't be afraid, don't worry, feel the love and joy of returning to the divine. On this final journey, you can find peace, solace, and guidance from your angel if you just open yourself up to the experience. If you have cultivated a relationship with your angel for many years, your crossing over will be that much easier because your angel comes to you as a dear old friend, not as a surprise or a shock. This healer, parent, and guide will hold you, love you, and help you make that last great transition into spirit.

READY, WILLING, AND ABLE TO MAKE FULL CONTACT!

Have you ever been thinking of a loved one and had them suddenly call? Have you every wanted to communicate a message to someone ("I hope my husband picks up milk on the way home") and had them almost miraculously act on your wish? The mind is a powerful and mysterious force! When you ask for divine guidance or some kind of practical help and the universe delivers, it amazes you. These things may seem like coincidences, but you may be amazed at how perfect these answers to your prayers really are. If you ask for divine help and something happens to give it to you once, maybe it is coincidence. But what if it happens over and over?

If you yearn for contact with your angel, if you concentrate on your desire for contact, you are already on your way. Your powers of concentration and imagination are key to this communication. If you feel ready, then you are ready. If you can feel the love of your Guardian Angel and in turn feel love for your angel, then you have found the most important key. If you have firmly decided that it is your will to meet and know your Guardian Angel, then it will happen. Of this there is no doubt. The most powerful way to prepare yourself to meet your Guardian Angel is simply to yearn for this contact with all of your mind, body, and soul. If you honestly reach a point where you feel this, where the influence and the touch of your angel seem present, but just out of sight and out of reach, then you are ready to connect with your Guardian Angel.

Chapter 3:

Contacting Your Guardian Angel

How can you connect with the angel that watches over you? If God has indeed assigned you a divine messenger, where do you start in your quest to reach out and grab your angel's hand? It is easier that you think!

First, you must acknowledge that there are spiritual dimensions or ways of seeing reality that differ from your day-to-day material existence. If you are convinced that the only reality is physical, then you have created a wall of disbelief that your angel cannot climb over. You have created a prison of doubt from which you must escape if you are to see out of the windows of your soul and communicate with the angel who patiently awaits you just beyond the limits of your perception.

I have heard many people describe how their Guardian Angels were always there, but just out of reach, until they made an effort to make contact. How did they break through the barrier between the physical world and the higher spiritual world? By calling upon their angels to change their perceptions, by changing their way of seeing and, most importantly, by taking a deeper look at their own identities!

If you think of the spirit world as consisting of higher levels of vibration or energy, then spiritual or psychic phenomena make sense. Psychics are simply people who, through training, talent, or both, can experience ranges of energy that most of us cannot. And they are not alone! If you have a dog or cat, you have probably watched them intently observing things that you couldn't see. My dog used to bark at a place on our stairway over and over, yet we could never see anything there. I myself have walked into places with my child that were "spooky," only to have him cry and urge me to leave. Yet there was nothing there—nothing I could see anyway! If you can open your mind enough to accept that these things are possible, then you are ready to take the next step!

Here is a short exercise designed to let you contact and experience directly the power and love of your Guardian Angel. Experience is the great teacher!

Exercise 4: Connecting with Your Guardian Angel

You will need a white candle and some salt. Go somewhere quiet where you will not be disturbed. Toss a little of the salt about you. Imagine all negative energies and thoughts flying away. Light the candle and pray to God in whatever manner you like that your mind may be open to the divine and that you may communicate with your Guardian Angel. It is best that you make your own prayer, but it can be something like this:

God, energy and light that pervades all things
May I become open to seeing the divine in all things and places
May I be open to accepting the divine in my life
May I be open to receiving guidance and help from my Guardian Angel
By your love and will that you give to me, so may it be.

Sit quietly for a few moments and open yourself to the divine light and energy around you. Breathe deeply and feel the light fill you. You are opening yourself as a flower opens in the sunlight. Now, ask for a touch from your Guardian Angel. What you are doing is opening your mind and your energetic body to contact with the divine, you are opening yourself to perceive levels of reality to which you were previously blind! When you are done, absorb all the light and energy into your body. Sprinkle salt about to cleanse the area, and blow out the candle.

Sue did this exercise for a week and suddenly became aware of a number of negative and positive things about her workplace. Certain areas repelled her. One place made her feel warm and comfortable whenever she sat there. She also began to sense the moods and feelings of her coworkers before they said anything to her. In short, she became more sensitive and soon her coworkers began to come to her with their problems! She changed careers and is now a therapist. Though she accepted the guidance of her Guardian Angel in this matter, simply becoming more aware and sensitive to others was enough for her! She is doing her work, the work that her Guardian Angel is here to help her with, and she feels content with that.

You will see that, simply by opening yourself to the energies about you, the divine in all things, what the ancients called magic, you can change your life in a way that satisfies you! As you do this, take the opportunity to think really carefully about what it is you need in life.

Notice that I did not say "what you want in life." The reason is simple. Wants or desires are created by the ego, by your false sense of self that has been shaped by your surroundings and who you have been told you are from birth. We are all in a constant state of wanting, and something as simple as a TV commercial can influence what we want. How many times has a soft drink commercial come on and made you thirsty? How often have you discovered that you wanted something just because a friend or neighbor bought that very thing? Although wanting things is not bad, confusing wanting or desiring with *needing* can completely skew your life and send you in directions that do not make you happy. You can end up in a constant state of dissatisfaction, of unhappiness, convinced that buying this or that will somehow help.

You are constantly being manipulated, pulled this way and that way by your transitory desires. You may want something very badly, then the next day or next week, you want something different. You run to and fro, always feeling rushed and yet often not really satisfied by what you accomplish! In this chaos of constantly shifting desires, you may occasionally have moments of calm when you are aware that you are being manipulated by others. This can cause despair, frustration, and anger, but can also be an opportunity for you to get some real guidance, a real "reality check."

Your Guardian Angel is ready to reach out a steadying hand to you through this whirlwind of thoughts, desires, worries, and illusions, but first you have to become still and discover who you are. In fact, if you want to achieve anything of worth, if you want to find and embody the divine plan you are meant to manifest, then you must first discover something essential—something you knew as a child but have forgotten in the years of growing up and listening to those around you. You have to rediscover who *you* are.

To reach for the heavens, you must first have your feet planted firmly on the Earth. Your Guardian Angel is a reflection of you, a glowing divine energy light, a ray of God connecting the divine to Earth. It is wholly part of you as you are part of it. By looking at yourself, you will begin to see your angel, but only if you see yourself as you really are! By knowing yourself, by delving deeper and deeper into your own personal identity, you will draw closer and closer to your Guardian Angel. This is the first step to self-realization, and this is the journey your Guardian Angel yearns for you to make. Remember: As within, so without!

STEP 1: KNOW YOURSELF

In ancient times, the rediscovery of self was called "The Great Work." Years of leading workshops has taught me that the work of self-discovery is the starting point of spiritual and physical transformation. All problems exist to teach you something and they often pass away or disappear when you have fully learned the lesson they are there to teach. Your Guardian Angel is the arbitrator of these lessons. Simply by reexamining who you are, you may make all sorts of breakthroughs physically, emotionally, and mentally, as well as spiritually. This is never easy, but it is always worth it! In fact, it is the true spiritual quest.

One note of caution: As you truly look at yourself and who you are with a new focus and clarity, you will find things that are painful and that make you uncomfortable. While these aspects of yourself may be hard to face, it is by confronting them that you will grow stronger, evolve, and become aware of obstacles that may have held you back. By objectively examining your strengths, weaknesses, goals, dreams, and fascinations, you begin to understand your Guardian Angel as a cosmic mirror of your own true self. By looking back over your life, you can see patterns, constellations of things and places and ideas that gave you true joy and spiritually empowered you. You can also reexamine your life through a new lens, and so become ready to fully receive your Guardian Angel.

As you perform this next exercise, remember that you are going to examine yourself as a whole, including all the positive and negative aspects of your being. Don't ignore your negative characteristics, but don't dwell on them either! God made you the way that you are; this is how you need to examine yourself.

Exercise 5: Examining Your Self (Body, Heart, Mind)

Set aside at least an hour to be alone with peace and quiet. You will need a pad of paper, three regular envelopes, and a pen or pencil.

Sit in a comfortable chair or on the floor in a dimly lit room and be completely still. Close your eyes, breathe quietly, and relax. Now, open your eyes. Think about who and what you are. Think about your whole life, from your earliest memories until the present. Ignore all the thoughts swirling about in your mind. Focus on the task.

After a few minutes, take a piece of paper. Write at the top: **Body**. Now, write your full name on the paper, followed by your birth date and all the statistics you can think of about yourself: height, weight, skin, hair, eyes. Build a clear and comprehensive description of yourself. This can all be done with lists. No one else will read this, so be completely honest in every way! You may have to stop and think about some of these things—we all take so much for granted and ignore so much of who we are! If you are not sure of how much you weigh, find out! If you have never thought of your eye color, go take a long careful look! You may be surprised! Green eyes, for example, can be dark green, light green, olive green, bluish green . . . look carefully at who you are! Do *not* write what others say about you. Write only what you see and know.

Continue describing your body. Write about each of your body parts: legs, arms, feet, hands, sexual organs, head, back—everything. Be honest and complete. When you simply cannot add any more to a physical description of yourself, describe the types of clothing you like to wear. What kinds of clothing do you prefer? What sorts of jewelry? Makeup? Shoes?

Finally, write what expressions you often have on your face and describe your common body language. Do you smile a lot? Frown a lot? Are you mostly slow-moving or do you rush everywhere? Close your eyes. Run through your average week. What do you see yourself doing? Watching TV? Drinking beer? Rollerblading? Swimming? Playing chess? Reading a novel? Write down all your habits, the things you are most likely to do. When you are done, fold the paper and put it into one of the envelopes. Write **Body/Action** on it. Set it aside.

Take another piece of paper and write at the top **Heart**. Now, write all the emotions you commonly feel with a few comments or words after each emotion to show what triggers it. For example, you might write:

Love:
Mom, Dad, Sis, my wife, my son, my uncle and aunt, my friends, pets, hiking, skiing, sunsets, etc.

Of course, it is impossible to write down everything you love or hate, or everything that causes you sadness or anger, but try to list the most important things. This is possibly the hardest part of this exercise. You may not readily be aware of all the things that, for example, make you angry. You must really dig into yourself.

On this page, list all the things that attract you and repel you. This includes common (or favorite) sexual fantasies as well as hidden fears (spiders, heights, etc.) Again, remember, no one will read this but you, and if you can't be honest with yourself, who can you be honest with?! When you are finished to the best of your ability, fold the paper or papers up and put them in an envelope. Mark the envelope with **Heart/Will** and set it aside.

Finally, take a fresh piece of paper and, at the top, write **Mind**. On this paper write all the things you know. That is, list the things you know about and things you know how to do. Begin with simple things (swim, read, ride a bike) and work your way up to more unusual skills (speak Spanish, sail a boat) with a focus on things that you are proud of or worked hard to master. Don't try to list everything you can do; write down those things that you have really developed your mind to be able to do. Think of this as an in-depth description of who you are and, in this case, how you think and what you know. Anything having to do with your mind and what is in it is fine! When you are done, fold the paper(s) and put them in the third envelope. Write **Mind/Knowledge** on it and set it with the other two.

When you are finished with the task, relax. Breathe deeply and say a prayer of thanks for self-knowledge. Thank the divine for making you so wonderful and complex! Spend a few minutes just letting your mind wander. It is likely that a number of things you have never spent much time contemplating will suddenly come to mind. You may realize things about yourself that are both good and painful. Let them all go. You are who you are and your Guardian Angel loves you no matter what!

When you feel it is time to end the exercise, place the three envelopes in the large envelope and put it in a hidden place where no one can find it. Leave it there for at least two weeks.

Now comes the fun part! When this time has passed, again set aside at least an hour with the pad and pen or pencil and your envelopes. Make sure that you will not be disturbed. Open each envelope and read the contents, but *read as if you were another person!* Who is this person you are reading about? What can you learn about them? What type of person is this? What does this person like and dislike? What does this person do? Feel? Think? In short: Who is this person?

When you have read all three envelopes carefully, write a short paragraph describing this person (you!) as if you were describing someone you knew to a future employer! Summarize! What patterns do you see emerging from this person's life? What makes this person feel fulfilled? If God has a plan for this person, what would it be? The summary must be less than half a page long! Now, read your summary to yourself out loud. This is *you.*

When you have finished, stop and be still. Ask yourself what patterns you see in your life. Why do you think you were put on this planet? What does God want you to do? Now, think carefully. How has the divine affected your life? You know who you are now. But what has made you who you are? This is the next step in your journey of self-realization.

By recognizing points in your past when you successfully followed divine inspiration, you can see how and where and when your Guardian Angel has been guiding you, even when you were unaware. Your angel has been communicating with you since birth, but now you can really begin to understand its messages. Synchronicities (meaningful coincidences), symbols, dreams, music, art, and what other people say and do in your life are all means your Guardian Angel uses to communicate with you.

If it is true that you have been guided by loving and invisible hands all of your life, why didn't you know it at the time? Why were you unaware of these moments of guidance, of divine help and support? You were probably either too close to the situation or were not looking! Cultures that teach children that the wonders of God are always around them produce children that can see such miracles all the time! You create your view of the universe around you by accepting what you have been taught as real and rejecting what you have been taught is impossible. If you are told something is impossible, if the very possibility of something is not even imaginable, then you will never see it. I once had a student tell me that he did not believe in ghosts because, if he did, they would come and bother him! I'm not too sure about ghosts, but his lack of logic actually contains a profound truth: Belief makes things possible.

STEP 2: KNOW YOUR LIFE

There is a pattern to the universe, a plan, an organizing principle that many call God. All things, including you, are a part of this unfolding plan, part of the universal pattern, and life and death are merely part of this plan. Your Guardian Angel can help you understand and follow your part of the universal plan. The following exercise can help you begin to see the patterns in your life. You will again need your pad of paper, a pen or pencil, and some quiet time, as well as the summary and other lists you wrote in Exercise 5.

Exercise 6: Examining Your Life

Go through your entire life and think deeply about every year. Feel free to refer to the summary and other lists you have already written. Don't write down everything that happened to you—that would make this a very large project! Instead, start with your birth and briefly note the following things if they happened to you:

- Moments of great clarity or amazement
- Moments of incredible joy or love
- Moments of deepest sorrow or trauma
- Near-death experiences or serious accidents
- "Aha!" moments of faith or great understanding
- Important chance encounters or coincidences that changed your life
- Moments when you made key decisions that changed your life
- Times when your intuition warned you about something that happened
- Times you escaped from injury or serious problems by luck
- Any other moments of great luck
- Any major or minor miracles that happened in your life

Take your time. This is a very important exercise and it may take you a number of days to finish. There may be events in your early childhood that you simply don't remember, but about which you have been told. For example, my mother accidentally let go of my stroller on a hill when I was an infant. It was only by extreme luck that a passerby leapt forward and grabbed it as it was about to career into traffic! This is a story I only found out about by chance while chatting with my mom on the phone!

When you are done with your list, sit quietly and think about this: During these key moments or points in your life, did you feel guidance or protection that was divine? Did you feel what is commonly called "the hand of God?"

Step out of yourself for a moment. Consider the point of view of an angel whose assignment is to help the person whose life is spread out before you, but to do so in a gentle, nonintrusive manner. Do you begin to see a pattern here? From what things were you diverted? Toward what things were you encouraged? What great moments of insight hit you? What happened in your life as a result? How did your intuition help or save you or someone else? What problems or accidents occurred when you did *not* listen to your intuition? ("I *knew* I shouldn't have done that...")

What emerges from your paper may startle you. You will begin to see a pattern, a plan, a series of instances of luck and coincidence and intuition that link together to form a purpose. One at a time, they can be ignored. Together, they reveal the framework of your life. In this pattern, this plan, you will see the face of your Guardian Angel!

With your pen, place a star next to each incident or event that you now believe was a direct result of divine guidance. Think about how your life has been shaped by this pattern. Look at the dead-ends and missed opportunities, the self-destructive or negative decisions that you made. Notice how there were attempts to steer you away for these negative choices? It is likely in these situations that your ego managed to push your Guardian Angel aside (we will discuss this more later).

As the pattern of connection between your Guardian Angel and your life is revealed, you need not accept it as objectively true, only as possible. Accepting the possibility of divine guidance and care is the first real step toward accepting that your Guardian Angel is as real as anything else and that you have had a divine protector with you since you were born. The point of Exercise 6 is to give you some things to look for in your life from now on, some hints that will help you recognize the pattern of when your Guardian Angel is trying to guide you or communicate with you. Think of it as "tuning in" to a higher wavelength or signal than you are used to hearing.

Upon reflection, you will see that many of the contacts you have had in the past with your angel have been seen as amazing hunches, as coincidence, or as the voice of intuition.

STEP 3: PAY ATTENTION

Teachers of all faiths tell us that the divine is speaking to us all the time, but we are often not listening. When you accept that your Guardian Angel, your personal connection to the divine, is indeed speaking to you all the time, you are halfway there! But listening to and understanding your angel are two very different things. It does no good to know that someone is talking to you if you cannot comprehend them.

The key to understanding your angel is simply to pay attention. Attention, or what is called "right-mindedness," is the most important element in connecting with the divine. Think of yourself as a child who is playing intently, not paying attention to what your parent is saying. Why? Because you are focusing on something else, something more interesting to you at the moment, something that probably engages your senses so that you shut out other things and people. We do this all the time. We tune people out and ignore noises that we do not want in our reality at the moment. Think about the last time someone who finally got your attention said, "Where was your mind just now?!"

You have been taught, subtly, by our culture and society to tune out voices, intuitions, and other phenomena that are not acknowledged as real. As a result, you have lost your sensitivity and your ability to understand communication on a higher spiritual level, though you were born with this ability. This is why children can contact their angels easily and experience higher levels of reality and magical energy. They haven't yet been taught that they can't! This is why Guardian Angels often appear as imaginary playmates until the children are taught that such things are illusion and thus not real.

In seeking to communicate with your Guardian Angel, your goal becomes to recreate the state of innocence and open-minded acceptance of the magical that you had as a child. You must try to reconnect with your invisible playmate, who never really left you. This invisible friend did not disappear, nor did you grow out of seeing him or her. You were pulled away from the loving connection you had with them by parental insistence and social disbelief. Nonetheless, this spirit has been patiently abiding with you all these years, helping and guiding you like a protective parent, even though you have tuned it out and focused on your day-to-day life in the physical world of sensations and material things. The next two exercises will help you reconnect with this companion of your younger, more innocent, days.

Exercise 7: Meeting Your Guardian Angel—The Staircase

Do this exercise in your bedroom or in another place that is quiet and warm, where you can lie down without being bothered for an hour or so. The place should have low lighting or even just a candle or two.

Breathe deeply and relax your body. Now, consciously relax each part of your body as you breathe deeply and slowly in and out:

Relax your feet; take off your shoes and totally relax.
Relax your ankles; pretend that they are no longer there. Feel every muscle relax!
Relax your legs.
Relax your thighs.
Relax your loins.
Relax your lower back completely.
Relax your upper back.
Relax your stomach; just let go.
Relax your chest; just relax.
Relax your arms; they are light…
Relax your shoulders; they have never been so relaxed…
Your neck is so relaxed—it never felt so great.
Relax your head; your head no longer feels like a part of you.
Relax all your face muscles… now your whole body is relaxed and light as a feather…

The peace you now feel can always be with you. Breathe slowly but do not fall asleep! You will now go on a mental journey to a special beautiful place where your Guardian Angel waits for you! Close your eyes and visualize a spiral staircase. Imagine a light up at the top of these stairs. At the top of the stairs is a door.

Walk up the stairs: first step, second, third, fourth, fifth, halfway there, sixth, seventh, eighth, ninth, tenth. Look at the door before you. It is open a little; there is light coming from behind it. Examine the door carefully until it is completely clear to you and as real as can be. Now, open the door and walk through.

You are in a beautiful place that is amazing and yet familiar; isn't it lovely? It is a special place for you. Enjoy it, sit and simply soak up the beauty. Call with all your love and will to your Guardian Angel.

At this point, you will have a personal experience with your angel. Ask any questions you want, but make sure to ask your angel to strengthen the bond between you. Tell your Guardian Angel that you wish to understand more. Then say goodbye to your angel. Remember that it is always with you and will never leave you, all you have to do is ask it to come and it will.

Get up, go to the door, and open it. You see the stairs in front of you with a small light at the bottom. Carefully descend. Take one step, say good-bye; second step, third, fourth. . .you are leaving. Fifth step, you are halfway down. Sixth step, seventh, you are almost home. Eighth, you are getting closer. Ninth, tenth, you are home. You are back in your body. Feel you arms, legs, back, and all parts of your body. When you open your eyes, you will feel relaxed and good, and will from now on have a closer relationship with your Guardian Angel. Now, record your experiences in a journal.

I have led many people through this exercise and, as simple as it sounds, it has sometimes had remarkable, life-changing effects! I recommend that you tape this simple visualization exercise and listen to it while lying down in a quiet place. It is also quite easy to do for a friend or loved one by quietly and slowly reading it aloud. Never do this without completing the exercise, and do your best never to be interrupted.

I've had several people burst into tears when they made contact with their Guardian Angels in this way. Several affirmed love relationships they had not been sure of, and, in at least five situations I can remember, people changed careers after doing this exercise just one time! Others had difficulty getting up the stairs, several could not get the door open, and many enjoyed their private beautiful place, but did not contact their Guardian Angels, although they did feel a presence. What does this mean? That we are all different and all in different stages of spiritual growth and learning. I have found that it often takes two or three repetitions for this exercise to be successful, especially if you have no experience with meditation or visualization. I have never found anyone who did this exercise several times who did not get something significant out of it.

In this next exercise, you will confront your Guardian Angel in a different way, calling on your own identity to make the connection. You will need a quiet, softly lit place to sit and relax for an hour or so. You will need to be seated in front of a mirror so that you can see at least your face clearly.

Exercise 8: Meeting Your Guardian Angel—The Mirror

When you are comfortable and relaxed, do the following:

Close your eyes and relax.
Breathe in. Hold. Breathe out. Hold. Do this for five minutes.
Completely relax. With every inhalation, you are filled with white light.
With every exhalation, breathe out cloudy-gray stress and negativity.
Relax and be filled with light.

Pray in whatever manner you like, asking God to help you see and connect with your Guardian Angel. Then slowly open your eyes and see the mirror before you. You see yourself. Look into your eyes. Your face is calm. *Think* this phrase over and over:

Self is self, Angel appear,
Reflection reveal, make it clear

You see an aura of energy about your reflection. Soon your reflection begins to glow. It begins to change. It becomes your self, and yet not your self. It is glowing with a pure light. It is smiling, it is beautiful. It is beaming love at you.

When this new image becomes clear and stops changing, stop your silent repetition of the phrase. Ask your Self/Guardian Angel for a symbol, a sign, or a name. It will be given to you.

When you are ready to end this, touch the mirror with both hands. The angelic reflection reaches out to meet you. Feel the light fill you; feel the energy of love fill you; feel your angel fill you. Then the reflection changes again, until it is again just a reflection of you. But you are smiling and filled with light.

This is a very powerful exercise that, again, may not be completely successful the first time you do it. Yet simply repeating it several times will produce remarkable effects on you. I have seen remarkable results from this exercise. Virtually everyone senses a light about and in them, and sees something higher and more beautiful in their reflection after only a short time. You may initially experience some fear as your reflection goes through many shifts and changes, but if you continue to focus with all your will on your Guardian Angel and on the goodness within you, this is what will always emerge.

This exercise helps you merge with and become closer to your divine self, your Guardian Angel. Your angel works through you to help you and to help you help others, which is why we are here on this Earth. By becoming more open, more receptive, and more accepting of your Guardian Angel, you become a better person and do more good in the world. Isn't that what it is all about?

These exercises, no matter how effective, are just the first steps on your journey. Feel free to do them as often as you like. Once you know who you are, accept the patterns of the divine in your life, and begin paying attention to your Guardian Angel, then the real fun begins!

Part 2:

Your Guardian Angel and You—
Deepening the Connection

Chapter 4:

Nurturing Your Angelic Connection

Like any seed that has been planted, the sprout of divine contact requires care to take root and flourish. To establish communication with your Guardian Angel and then ignore it is ultimately self-defeating. Nurturing and cultivating your relationship with your Guardian Angel, while amazingly rewarding in all aspects of your life, takes effort, just like any other relationship. Moreover, like a new seed, it requires certain elements to succeed: sunlight (the light of consciousness), water (the power of positive emotions), and soil (the strength of a pure body). Only when these three elements coexist can you reap the full benefits of your Guardian Angel's presence.

SUNLIGHT: THE LIGHT OF CONSCIOUSNESS

Constant watchfulness is the key to strengthening your link with your Guardian Angel. Attentiveness and awareness are the most powerful tools you have for evolving spiritually and for really understanding what your Guardian Angel is trying to say to you. The more aware you are of your surroundings, the more your Guardian Angel can use the vast canvas of reality to communicate with you.

Awareness is the key to any spiritual advancement. Your Guardian Angel will help you experience compassion for all living things, especially for your fellow human beings, and lead you to an inner awareness that all nature is connected and part of a vast cosmic pattern.

Think of the universe as one unified being—God, if you will—composed of life, energy and, more than anything, consciousness. The only thing that separates you from animals and plants in terms of real spirituality is your consciousness. You know when you do right and wrong, whereas a patch of poison ivy doesn't know that it causes harm to those who touch it and an attack dog doesn't realize that it is doing wrong by biting someone it feels is a threat to its owner. Animals, and to a lesser extent plants, operate by instincts and life patterns given directly to them in their genetic code. When they are born, they seek food, survival, and the means to reproduce. They don't question this state of affairs; they don't ponder the meaning of their life cycle or why they are here. Simple existence is enough for them and the search for survival and pleasure is sufficient to justify their existence.

Human beings are different. For many reasons that can be debated endlessly, we are all in various stages of awareness. The least aware simply live life in their animal natures. They live for survival, pleasure, to amass territory and goods, and they view all things in terms of how they personally benefit from or are negatively impacted by them. These people are selfish, self-centered, greedy, and uncaring of others. We all know people like this. They are essentially unaware and uncaring of the effect they have on others, on society, or on their environment. Their immediate needs, desires, and gratification come first, all else second. Self-righteous, close-minded, and unable to compromise, these people are essentially responsible for much of the world's misery, war, and pollution.

The most aware people are easy to spot in any country around the world. They are the saints, holy men and women, the ones willing to give all, even their lives, to help others in need. Their awareness and consciousness is so wide and open that it encompasses all of creation and all of this world. They are as open and selfless as the least aware are closed and self-centered. They are the Ghandis, the Mother Teresas, the Schindlers, and Dalai Lamas of this world. Most of us fall somewhere in the middle: neither base animal, nor saint.

All the great prophets and teachers, including Buddha, Jesus, and Mohammed, gave instructions to their followers on how to become an aware and open person who literally "loves their neighbors as themselves." Some of their directives include:

- Love everyone as you love yourself.
- Be as a child (open, aware, accepting) and you will have the keys to heaven.
- Do good deeds, help the poor and sick, share what you have.
- Avoid hurting others and never kill.
- Forgive completely those less aware than you, even if they hurt you.
- Avoid envy, jealousy, and attachment to things.
- Accept that you are divine, follow what this divine force leads you to do.
- Accept that all beings are divine, treat them this way.
- While accepting your animal or base nature, do not let it enslave you.

All of these instructions can be synthesized into one simple phrase: Become more aware. Awareness or consciousness is a form of knowledge beyond the simple intellectual learning of facts and figures. It is more than simply knowing about the people and things around you; it is a deep and hard-to-pin-down concept that the ancients referred to as *gnosis*, or inner knowing. True awareness comes when you seek to experience reality beyond the narrow box of your ego, when you seek to perceive and comprehend the true nature of the world around you, both physically and spiritually.

How can you actively seek to expand your awareness? How can you become more conscious? Isn't this the true spiritual path of every faith, the quest for greater consciousness? Fortunately, you have a guide or teacher that is prepared to lay out the specific steps you must take to become more aware, more conscious. God is the entire universe—the life force that pervades and enlightens all things, the ultimate consciousness—but there is a spark of awareness of this consciousness within you. As the galaxy is full of infinite stars, so you have a star within you, a Sun to which you naturally gravitate just as a newly sprouted seed seeks the solar rays with its leaves. As a small child, you are supremely confident. You *know* things, you feel protected and are fully aware that reality is flexible and very much what you make it. As you grow up, these notions are taken away from you and you are taught to rely on external guides: parents, relatives, teachers, the media, or friends. The inner guide or invisible playmate who proffered such a pure view of the world—what we call innocence—is pushed to the side, called imaginary and actively discouraged. Yet your Guardian Angel has not left you at all, as story after story shows.

True consciousness or awareness is beyond the narrow view of the real accepted by most people. All the great spiritual teachers tell us this, that the real world is just a beginning place, that spiritual things, emotions, greater truths, and other intangibles are far more important in the long run than physical objects and narrow notions. Yet these narrow views of reality are comforting. It is difficult, challenging, and sometimes even painful to open up your view of reality and spirituality. It often means giving up parts of your self, your ego, to a greater truth. Yet your Guardian Angel stands ready to help you become a more conscious, a more human, being. In fact, your Guardian Angel is constantly giving you specific instructions and guidance that you may be ignoring every day. To become more aware, you must begin to heed these messages.

To understand this, you will have to shift your view of reality for a moment. Because of the enormous amount of data coming into your brain via your senses, your brain plays many games and takes many shortcuts. It assumes many things and jumps to conclusions. How many times have you seen a friend on the street only to find out that, as you got closer, it wasn't really who you thought it was? All the clues were there, so your brain jumped to the conclusion it was your friend. This is why stage magic is so effective, because you are not really conscious of all that is going on. Your mind is so busy and processing so much that it rarely turns its full attention to anything. Have you ever gone into the same room or office so many times that you don't really see it anymore? If something is moved or something is changed you probably won't notice it. Carry this idea a little further: How much of what goes on around you do you really catch? I recently went to a lecture on autism, something that is important to me, and the professor talked about taping a session with an autistic boy who kept staring off into the distance. She thought it was just part of his disorder, until she replayed the tape. There it was, though she had completely missed it at the time, two birds singing beautifully. The autistic child had caught it however, because children with autism simply do not have the mental filters we take for granted. They are hypersensitive because they are unable to screen out all the distractions and stimuli that constantly bombard the rest of us. You, on the other hand, unconsciously screen out most of what goes on around you in order to accomplish the task at hand. Your ego decides what you need to do (make dinner, get dressed, do your job) and stimuli that does not pertain to this focus is screened. This is why, when you are reading, you often do not hear people who attempt to talk to you! It is a perfectly normal and natural state of affairs that keeps you on task and helps you survive!

If you want to become more aware, more conscious, so you can receive the knowledge (gnosis!) that your Guardian Angel is constantly trying to give you, you have to find a way to work around the blinders that your ego places on your ability to perceive reality about you. This technique, as simple as it sounds, is called contemplation or meditation. Every mystical religion practices it. What they do not tell you, however, is that the technique does not depend on belief to be successful; focus and willpower will suffice. Meditation, if done properly, is a tool that can open you up to receiving communication from your higher Self.

Exercise 9 (see following page) describes a method for expanding your awareness in order to understand messages from your Guardian Angel. Its basic goal is to raise your vibration level closer to that of your Guardian Angel so that communication becomes easier and clearer. This exercise makes several assumptions. The first is that you must reach for union with the ultimate (God, etc.) one step at a time. The first step in the path to union with the divine is to connect with the inner spark of God that is within you, your Guardian Angel. As you meditate and reach upward (or inward, depending on your point of view), so does your Guardian Angel reach and strain toward you! In fact, one of the first key truths about the Guardian Angel is that, for every step you take toward your Guardian Angel, it takes a step toward you. Thus, meditating on your angel is simpler than most traditional meditations. You just have to start the process and your angel will do most of the work for you, and be overjoyed to do so!

Using meditation to connect with your Guardian Angel sidesteps one of the major pitfalls of meditation in general—the depression or sadness that sometimes sets in when you touch the divine and realize how inadequate your small human abilities are to conceiving such a presence. But God has given you a personal connection to the divine, a being who will always answer your prayers and questions. This is your Guardian Angel. Those who do not hear God are simply looking too high, for the word of God is standing beside you at this moment and for the rest of your life!

This meditation exercise will open your awareness and raise your consciousness as well as your energy level. It will invite the presence of your Guardian Angel into your daily life and remove the veils that have blinded you to its constant presence. Is that worth ten minutes once or twice a day? Try it and find out!

One last thing: *I strongly advise that you keep a simple journal as you start down this path.* There are several reasons for doing this. First, it signals to your self and to your Guardian Angel that you are serious about this process. Second, your angel will very quickly begin to communicate with you and it is very important that you write down your thoughts, dreams, and messages, because many of them will only make sense later on. Without a record, you may forget. Indeed, increasing awareness is all about remembering! Finally, by keeping notes you will be able to track your progress and see clearly how your consciousness and your relationship with your Guardian Angel is growing and blossoming.

Exercise 9: Meditating on Your Guardian Angel

Perform this meditation for about ten minutes once or twice a day as you like. You will need a quiet time when you will not be disturbed, and relaxing, comfortable clothes and surroundings.

Sit in a comfortable chair, at a time when you will not be disturbed. You should be completely relaxed and comfortable and should not have taken any kind of drug, including coffee, tobacco, or even large amounts of sugar. Morning is often the best time for this, though evening is also a good time.

Relax and breathe deeply and rhythmically, sometimes counting in and out. Focus on your breathing and release your mind, letting thought processes and ego-babble simply run their course without attachment until your mind is quiet. You can sometimes achieve this through a single-minded focus on one specific thought, image, prayer, or sound to the exclusion of all others. When your mind is quiet, pray to the divine in whatever way you wish, in whatever tradition you are comfortable. Pray for the removal of obstacles, for self-knowledge, and for greater awareness.

See a ring of pure white light about you, protecting you from all harm and filling you with pure, white light that banishes all stress and negativity. Sit and breathe quietly. Breathe this white light into your body and feel yourself filled with it until you are completely at peace.

Relax and meditate like this for a couple of minutes. Let the normal mental babble and millions of stray thoughts flow through your mind. Do not seek to stop them, but withdraw from them, let them go like eddies on a river, simply ignore them and hold yourself as still as possible. Let your mind go but hold to the center of your being. This sounds strange, but you will experience what I am talking about. Relax, relax. If you are in any way uncomfortable, stop what you are doing and try again at another time. You cannot hurt yourself or in any way endanger yourself if you are meditating surrounded by divine light! Relax! When you are ready, breathe in deeply and silently say to yourself:

Guardian Angel, come to me.

Then exhale slowly and say to yourself:

With Love and Will, so may it be!

Pause, then repeat this breathing exercise for as long as you like—five minutes is wonderful—then let it fade away. Continue the slow breathing in and out and open your mind, heart, and body to your Guardian Angel. It will come. No matter what your see or feel, stay relaxed and centered. Do not become emotional or try to force the experience. This is meditation; you are passive and are not *doing* anything, simply accepting the experience.

When the communication is over—and you will know it when it is—simply pray in any way you feel comfortable to the divine, thanking God (or however you see the divine) for this gift and experience and asking for a constantly growing awareness of the divine and of your Guardian Angel! It is important that you let go of your desires and worldly thoughts during this meditation.

When you are done, again see yourself surrounded by white light and see it disperse or fade into Mother Earth. Slowly come back to the physical world and, before you forget, record your experiences in your journal!

Can you believe that only ten minutes have passed?! Isn't that amazing? This simple meditation will prepare you for connecting with your angel like nothing else. If you can manage to do this every day, you will gain remarkable results in just a week. The effects are cumulative, so persevere!

The overall goal of this meditation exercise is simply to open your mind to new possibilities and to messages from your angel. It serves to raise your awareness of what is going on around you so that you can heed the advice and guidance that your Guardian Angel is providing. Which leads us to another key truth about the Guardian Angel: *Your angel is speaking to you every day, but you are not always listening.* In other words, your meditations and growing awareness will not cause your Guardian Angel to communicate with you they will simply help you tune into the transmissions that your Guardian Angel is sending you all the time! Think of it as learning to hear the birds singing in your back yard. The birds have always been singing, you have just been too preoccupied with other things to stop and really listen!

As you do your meditation exercises—and you may find yourself doing them in different places at different times as the mood strikes—you must follow up by doing what is sometimes called "walking meditation" with your Guardian Angel. This simply amounts to being mindful of everything around you, to appreciating the beauty and joy of your world, clearly seeing and accepting the challenges that face you. Go beyond and behind the experiences of your daily life while walking to school or driving to work or taking the kids to soccer practice. Start really looking and listening for the presence and communications of the divine in everything around you!

Do not think that your Guardian Angel will speak to you in thunderclaps and grand visions. Guardian Angels guide gently. They communicate and (always) teach with the ultimate classroom materials: reality and perception. Become open to these communications by looking at everything and everybody as a possible means of communication between you and the divine, no matter how trivial it may seem. These communications may come to you as sudden urges, hunches, intuitive flashes, or coincidences. Examples range from the silly to the serious, but if you look you will see a pattern of guidance that reaches into all parts of your life. Think back on all the times that intuition and hunches have helped you, and all the times you knew you should or should not do something—and ignored that instinct to your sorrow!

The best way to open up to communication from your Guardian Angel is to really pay attention to your inner voice and to your reality. You must become more aware of the inner and outer ways that your Guardian Angel communicates with you. Start by really paying attention to sudden urges or unexplained feelings and intuitions that seem to pop out of nowhere. Learn to recognize the distinct quality of those hunches and inspirations that are indeed true and helpful. After a while, you will begin to recognize the touch or voice of your Guardian Angel, as opposed to mere stray thoughts and ego-desires. For one thing, these instincts are never mean or controlling; they are always simple and clear urges or suggestions that leave behind a distinctive flavor. Learn to recognize this and you will have become truly aware!

Coincidences and seemingly unrelated symbols or things are important. Your Guardian Angel will use any and all means to communicate with you. Angels speak using the language of reality, if you just observe! Aside from your inner voice or intuition, your Guardian Angel is always tossing you all sorts of clues in order to teach and guide. Sound silly?

Mystics from many religions speak of the divine speaking to us through the world. Reality is very much what we think it is, unconsciously and consciously. If you assign value or meaning to certain objects, symbols, or images, your Guardian Angel will use them to communicate with you. If this seems silly, remember that your Guardian Angel is using what is in your reality to communicate with you. This may include all sorts of mundane ideas and symbols. You will recognize the authenticity of the message by the characteristic "tingle" or "feeling" that accompanies it. This feeling—that certain "touch of the Guardian Angel" feeling—is something you will experience for yourself as you learn to trust your angel more and more.

Finally, your Guardian Angel speaks to you all the time through the words and actions of other people. How can this be? Are these people being controlled by your angel? It is an interesting question and one that is not so easy to answer. More likely your angel is simply helping you see or hear something someone else says or does in a certain way that is only meaningful to you, using your awareness or perception to show you something. Still, it cannot be denied that the divine often guides you through the inadvertent actions and words of others, if you are but aware enough to "get it!" The divine does move in mysterious ways!

WATER: THE NOURISHMENT OF EMOTION

In many ways what you feel at any given moment is the most powerful thing in your life. It colors all your perceptions and significantly alters your mood and thus your view of reality. Lovers see a rainstorm as romantic, but an irritated salesman sees it as a horror. The shift from viewing angels as abstract concepts to very real and very personal beings is imperative in the process of giving to and receiving from your angel. When you make an emotional connection with your angel, this becomes remarkably easy.

When you begin to love your Guardian Angel, you begin to have a fixed image of what that angel is like. You begin to see and feel its characteristics in a very real way. This process is the key to creating an effective connection and relationship. Without positive emotions and strong loving feelings, no relationship can last—and this is perhaps the most important relationship in your life. Just as everyone falls in love differently, everyone connects emotionally with their angels in different ways. The key, however, is always love.

The process of cultivating an emotional bond with your Guardian Angel can be visualized as the blooming of a rose. Not only does your connection with your angel become stronger, you, as the person nurturing this growing, loving bond, become happier, more open, more centered in all aspects of your life. When you love your angel, and that love is returned, your self-confidence and sense of self-worth increase, as well as your capacity for divine inspiration. The warmth of this loving bond will positively affect all areas of your life.

Just as your Guardian Angel guides, protects, and teaches you, it also heals, comforts, and nurtures you, but only if you are open to it. Just as you need to open your mind and increase your awareness of your perceptions and mental processes in order to tune in to your angel, you also need to open your heart in order to receive the comfort and love your angel offers you.

No one escapes this material world of suffering without experiencing pain and loss. All of us have reached points of emotional pain where we were devastated and could not go on. Yet in your darkest hours, if you pray or open yourself to divine help, you always receive some comfort, the feeling that someone deeply cares. I have often heard about people in extreme need being comforted by a presence, feeling hugged or touched by invisible hands, and being soothed by waves of love and caring from no apparent source. This is how your Guardian Angel communicates with you emotionally.

Every culture assigns this divine comforting and nurturing to a spirit, guardian, or angel specific to each person. The entity that comforts you in need must be *your* entity, because the way you are comforted, the thoughts and caring that fill you, are very personal indeed. They belong to *your* Guardian Angel, because only your angel cares about you more than anything else in the world. How wonderful is that?

Yet many deny themselves the emotional support, caring, and nurturing their Guardian Angels offer them all day, every day! Why? Mostly because, again, they are simply unaware. Remember the invisible friend you had when you were very young, before you were told to stop such "foolishness"? This friend, your Guardian Angel, was someone you could always go to with your troubles, someone who always provided support and comfort and solace. Well, open yourself to this idea: That kind of emotional support, healing, and comfort can be yours again if you simply accept the possibility of it! Just as you can never make someone your true friend or lover without opening your heart, so you can never establish a relationship with your Guardian Angel without first accepting that this is possible. When you open your heart to your Guardian Angel, you will receive love, comfort, and emotional support. Then you must return the favor.

When you feel blue or depressed, simply sit down, and do the Guardian Angel meditation described in Exercise 9 on page 35. When you feel the presence of your angel, tell it that you are feeling pain, suffering, loss, frustration, anger. Unload! Ask for comfort and love and guidance. You will get it. Make sure you have tissues ready! Your Guardian Angel is there for you; it will help you carry heavy burdens and find answers to emotional problems. *Your angel is pure love and is attracted to love and the need for love.*

What do you think is the surest and the fastest way to push your Guardian Angel away and guarantee that you will *not* receive the love and comfort you need in times of stress and pain? In your heart, you know the answer: If you turn to anger or hate, your Guardian Angel cannot help you. All spiritual beings, and especially angels, will be banished and sent packing if you project hate or anger. Where there is hate or anger, there will be no angels. If you are an excessively angry, hostile, or hateful person, you push your Guardian Angel away and wall off your heart from its love and support. Such a loss for a little bit of hateful satisfaction!

So, how can you open your heart and prepare yourself to accept the love and comfort your Guardian Angel offers? First, accept that you are worth loving, worth comforting, and in general a worthwhile human being who deserves happiness and nurturing. Accept that God truly loves you. This is often a very difficult thing for people to accept. If you cannot love yourself and do not feel worthy of love, your Guardian Angel cannot get through to you. You must believe in yourself for your angel to be able to connect with you. Poor self-esteem is difficult to overcome and it may require counseling for you to move beyond it. Or you may succeed by simply asking and praying for the ability to see yourself as a loving being deserving of love.

Next, you have to create a loving and positive atmosphere or environment around yourself. Surround yourself with what the Chinese call "positive *chi*" or positive energy.

This means "talking the talk and walking the walk" of a loving person. Practice fostering positive emotions as often as possible: happiness, contentment, peace, tranquility, humor, acceptance. There is no secret here. Even the physical sciences tell us that like attracts like. Does this mean you should suppress or ignore negative emotions like anger, hate, or irritation? Of course not. Yet you should not dwell on them or hold on to them; you should let them flow through you and, as much as possible, return to a "default" state of positive emotional balance.

Do a reality check on yourself for a week. Ask yourself several times a day: "Am I a positive person?" If the answer is mostly no, then you have problems with your attitude and your outlook that need to be worked on if you wish to become closer to your Guardian Angel.

It is easy to blame others or your surroundings for your unhappiness, but unless you were born with serious health problems or in dire poverty, you have no excuse for not finding a way to be generally content with your life. If you feel yourself becoming a negative person, find out why and change it! If your job makes you unhappy, find one that doesn't. If your living situation is to blame, move. In a bad relationship? Leave it and begin again. You may say that it's simply not that easy, but, in the end, change is always possible and is always preferable to becoming a bitter, unhappy person.

Don't like yourself? Ah, here is the real problem behind many of the other problems you may *think* you have. There actually is a fairly easy answer to being unhappy with yourself (your weight, your height, your complexion, and so on). Form a relationship with your Guardian Angel, for this is in many important ways the best of you, the part of you that is godlike. Strengthen your bond with your angel and you will become more like it every day. You will also become more and more aware of what a miracle you are and all you are capable of being. Then you can begin to love that new self more and more.

When all excuses are peeled away, you will begin to see things in a more positive light every day and you will remove one of the main obstacles that keeps you from getting closer to your Guardian Angel. How can you do this? Where do you start?

First, simply stop complaining! *No whining*, as the sticker says. It is astounding how much negative energy is generated every day by complaining and whining. Over a third of the world is in deep poverty, yet you had the money to buy this book. Really, do you have anything substantive to complain about? When you are faced with what you perceive as a serious problem, ask yourself this: In a year, will this problem still matter? In ten years?

Stop worrying so much! Anxiety and excessive worry never helped solve anything. Moreover, they have been proven to cause serious mental and physical problems. Anxiety, low-level fright, is a residual survival mechanism originally intended to keep us from being devoured by wolves. Nowadays, it is triggered by everything from a domestic fight to a dire headline in the newspaper. We have become addicted to stress and worrying! You are not powerless here. Simply take a few hours to unplug from everything and think long and hard about what makes you anxious. Then, focus on the spirit, on God, and on your Guardian Angel. In the center of your being is a stillness and peace that neither headlines nor deadlines can reach. Focus on what is *real*.

It takes tremendous effort and a leap of faith to confront the emotional complexity that surrounds your worries and fears. You build emotional fortresses around these feelings because they give you excuses for not having achieved what you could have. But the choice remains yours: worry needlessly, surround yourself with negative influences that sap your strength, and drive your Guardian Angel away—or take real steps to make yourself less of a nervous wreck!

Release your feelings of anger and hatred, difficult though that may be. Anger and hatred come from within and are direct results of pain and frustration. It is not within the scope of the book to teach anger management or convince you that tolerance is a more productive emotion than hate. There are many books that can do that. The fact is that, in the short term, anger feels good, it is very satisfying. When I hit my thumb with a hammer, I love to curse and throw the hammer on the ground. When a charity that supports handicapped children was defrauded, I was very angry. I hated the wrongdoers; they had done a terribly evil thing. Was my anger justified? My hate? Most would think so. But the fact remains that *feeling and expressing hate or anger is the surest way to keep your Guardian Angel from communicating its love and support to you.* In this context, it is significant that most of the world's religions hold these truths as central to their faiths: Avoid anger; accept what God gives you; and return hate with love.

As a person who is often challenged by feelings of anger and sometimes feelings of hate, I offer this advice. Do not expect that you will be able to rid yourself entirely of these feelings. It is unlikely that this will happen. Instead, when these emotions arise, let them pass through you and let go of them without passing them on to others through your words or actions. One angry person can poison the mood of a whole group, as everyone knows. Find ways that work for you to let anger and hateful feelings flow through you with minimal harm to yourself and others. And practice loving more!

Be thankful! Make an effort to view the fantastic world around you with more feelings of gratitude. On the way to work, admire the clouds, the trees, the mountains and flowers. Or maybe the neon signs, the way people walk, the sound of someone singing. Approach every day as if it were your last! Life is so wonderful, you have so much that many do not have. Appreciate what is around you. Siberian shamans whom I have met from the Ulchi tribe have a very simple view of the universe. To them, the greatest prayer you can make, one you should make with every step you take upon Mother Earth is this: Thankfulness. Appreciation. Gratitude.

Try this simple exercise. Be consciously thankful for everything good in your reality for just one day. Try it. Feel gratitude for the sunrise, the trees in your yard, the flowers by the fence, the music coming from your car radio, the delicious coffee you are drinking, the love you receive from your family and friends. Try it. It will change your world.

Love more. Your Guardian Angel—in fact, all angels—are pure love. Nothing is more attractive to your Guardian Angel than your emanating love. Open your heart and feel love for everything and everyone you can. All religions say it, but few practice it: Love thy neighbor as thyself. This is a very real formula of tremendous power, one that is simple and so very clear. Remember, each and every person has a Guardian Angel, a Higher Self. Even those who are not conscious of this and who act out of base desires and impulses have this spark of God within them. If you can find it within you to love the divine, you can extend this love to the divine that inhabits every person.

Do your best to beam, from your heart, love to all people. If you cannot do this, then at least try to avoid anger and hate. It is amazing, actually, what love can do. Imagine that lone protester in Tiananmen Square who faced down a column of tanks with just his will and the power of his love. Look at the mountains moved by Ghandi and Martin Luther King and many more. Your Guardian Angel is not asking for such sacrifices from you. It asks only that you try to offer love as often as possible, to as many people as possible, and that you avoid inflicting pain. In the end, this is what truly matters and what truly lasts. Hatred and anger fade; they do not create anything real except more hatred and anger. How can they? They drive away the divine. Only love endures. Deep down, everyone knows this, but we tend to ignore something so simple it seems self-evident. It begins with you. Offer love as often as possible. You will never regret it and you will be opening wide the doors of your heart to receive your Guardian Angel!

SOIL: CULTIVATING THE PHYSICAL TEMPLE FOR UNION WITH THE GUARDIAN ANGEL

Bodily sensations and actions are the "food" that feeds the angelic connection. A passive contemplation of ideals and images is fine for meditation. It clears your mind and gets you centered, but it is simply not enough. Your Guardian Angel is there to guide you and help you grow. But if you don't go out and get physically involved in life, if you don't "get on the boat and row," how can you be guided? A docked boat has no need of a captain or a first mate, just as a person uninvolved in the pains and joys of life has no real need or justification for calling upon his or her angel.

One woman I knew was intensely unhappy until she connected with her angel and received the advice to draw. When she finally listened to the repeated urgings of her angel and tried it, she blossomed as a person and ended up becoming a professional artist. The point is, by not being aware of the possibility of *physically doing* art, she could not follow her true will and accomplish what her angel was urging her to do. If you don't try things, if you don't *do things*, you'll never know if they are meant for you or not!

All such active work starts with the "soil" within which the "seed" of the divine is planted: your body. Your body is the temple of the divine. When you forge a bond between yourself and your Guardian Angel, this is especially true, although perhaps not immediately evident. In the past, holy men and women have believed that every blade of grass has an angel. Some modern mystics have postulated that every cell in your body likewise has an angel assigned to it. As silly as this may sound, you can look at your body as a network of cells that work together in harmony when you are well. This harmony breaks down, however, when all your cells do not work well together. A cancer cell is simply a cell that is out of control, one that is not working in harmony with your body as a whole. Thus harmony is crucial.

There is nothing new here. But I want to take this thought one step further. When I say that your Guardian Angel is watching over you, this is not some abstract concept. It is real and it includes your physical body as well as your mental and emotional states of being. Some spiritual groups tend to separate the physical and the spiritual, thus causing many serious social and emotional problems by ignoring the basic mind/emotion/body relationship. This approach can lead to the suppression of natural instincts—the need for pure food and water, sexuality, the healthy balance of the body—which are seen as secondary or removed from the spiritual state of a person. Thankfully, this is changing. Many churches and spiritual groups now include classes on diet, yoga, nutrition, stress relief, and sexuality. There is a growing awareness of a person as a *holistic* being whose spiritual health is closely related to its physical health. In the center of this balance and this natural harmony sits the Guardian Angel.

Just as your Guardian Angel is concerned about your spiritual evolution, so it is deeply concerned with your physical state. The reason is very simple. First, that's your angel's job! But on a more fundamental level, your Guardian Angel's primary function is to unite with you and help you as much as possible. And your physical being is the foundation or basis of your spiritual advancement. If your angel is repelled by a polluted temple, if your body is severely out of harmony (discounting accidents of birth or chronic illness), it cannot work closely with you.

Spirit is reflected in matter and matter in spirit. Your Guardian Angel always seeks harmony between the two. Does this mean that your angel will avoid you if you are ill or suffer from a chronic ailment? Of course not! The trials of the human body are many. There is a reason for everything, though life and the afflictions we suffer may often seem cruel and arbitrary. Illness is often not willed or deserved, it simply is. Yet the key here is indeed the *Will.* Your Guardian Angel responds to the will you embody—in this case, the will to maintain your body in harmony. In other words, the respect you show your body in some ways determines your relationship with your Guardian Angel.

In many cases, people with special needs have a natural affinity and closeness with their Guardian Angels. I would offer such public figures as Stephen Hawking as examples of genius flowering amid adversity. The difference is one of awareness—this time, awareness of your body. In order to attract your Guardian Angel, to create an optimal environment for a closer relationship with your angel, you should strive to be as physically balanced and have as much body harmony as possible. Here are some simple ways to accomplish that:

Maintain a healthy diet. Avoid, as much as possible, excess in eating, drinking, and substance use. Be moderate in anything you put into your body. Be aware of everything you take into it, including chemicals and additives. It is easy to simply eat and drink and remain ignorant of what you consume, but in spiritual practice as well as the law, ignorance is no excuse! Your body is *your* temple; you have custody of it. The more harmonious it is, the more welcome your Guardian Angel will feel!

Exercise on a regular basis. You do not have to be a body builder, but you should be as healthy and strong as possible. Find the weight that is comfortable for you. Often simply eating properly and exercising will bring you to where you want to be.

Get enough rest. This is so hard to do in our crazy world, and everyone has different needs, but if you stop and think about this with an open mind, you will know if you are feeling overtired and burned out. Simply taking more stimulants like coffee often compounds the problem.

Lower your stress level. This may be physical, mental, or emotional stress, depending on your life situation and your job. Meditation, exercise, Tai Chi, yoga, or hiking are all great ways to relieve stress. Find what works for you and make sure you continue the practice on a regular basis. Again, as with negative emotions or mental problems, the key is to let the stress flow through you, not to lock it in, repress it, or in any other way hold onto it.

The key to maintaining a healthy physical temple for your Guardian Angel is to heal the physical problems you can heal and accept the ones you cannot heal. Today you have an array of healthcare professionals, from doctors to naturopaths, who can help you heal your ills and maintain your physical health. My main advice here is to listen to your inner voice when it prompts you to attain health or heal yourself. Your Guardian Angel will try to alert you to health problems *before* they become serious. Listen! Your angel will also try to guide you toward the treatments and professionals you need, but you must be aware of this guidance no matter how it manifests in your life. No amount of guidance can help you if you do not listen and follow your health professional's advice! Combine physical medicines and procedures with meditation and prayer in your healing regimen. Call on your Guardian Angel to help heal you! Your spirit and body are intertwined. Healing one will help you heal the other.

Respect your body and your environment. Keep both clean and pleasing to the eye. This will improve your spiritual as well as your physical state. Keeping your physical surroundings and your body clean will also purify both spiritually. Feeling especially "yucky" after a nasty day at work? Had someone dump their stress on you? Feeling uneasy? Add a little salt to your bath water, sprinkle a little salt around your house, then sweep it up and toss it out. In dozens of different cultures, salt is used to purify and remove negative influences from the physical body or environment. Try it and see if it works! Aromatherapy and a number of other physical aids can be used as well. Consult your Guardian Angel. It will guide you to what you need!

These simple things can help you prepare yourself physically for a closer relationship with your Guardian Angel. Just as a battery needs to be constructed in a certain manner to receive and hold an electrical charge, your physical body needs to be as harmonious and balanced as possible to receive the spark of God that is your Guardian Angel. Exercise 10 is designed to purify or energize you body and help it rebalance itself. It can help you prepare your body to receive the higher energies of your angel. It is also excellent for healing, removing stress, alleviating fatigue, and in general helping your physical body become more healthy. I use the prayer word *OM* to signify the divine here. Feel free to use *Amen* or any other special word that signifies the divine in your faith.

Exercise 10: Empowering Your Body

Find a quiet place where you will not be disturbed for at least fifteen minutes. Somewhere outside near a tree is best, but anywhere comfortable and quiet will do. Sit still and breathe normally. Become aware of all the parts of your body as you steadily breathe in and out. Calm yourself and relax every part of you. See yourself surrounded by a ring of white light that drives away all negative feelings and thoughts.

Place your hands together and pray in whatever way you feel comfortable. Pray for healing, balancing, and purification of your body. Feel your hands become warm; they are filled with white light. Concentrate on your hands filled with light.

Ask your Guardian Angel to help you find health and balance now. As you place your hands on each body part, feel and see it infused with glowing white light. Place your hands on your right leg and say:

I heal and purify myself with the divine light, OM!

Place your hands on your left leg and say:

I heal and purify myself with the divine light, OM!

Place your hands on your right shoulder/arm and say:

I heal and purify myself with the divine light, OM!

Place your hands on your left shoulder/arm and say:

I heal and purify myself with the divine light, OM!

Place your hands on your loins/lower belly and say:

I heal and purify myself with the divine light, OM!

Place your hands on your heart and say:

I heal and purify myself with the divine light, OM!

Place your hands on your forehead and say:

I heal and purify myself with the divine light, OM!

Place your hands on top of your head and then bring them together in front of you and say:

I heal and purify myself with the divine light, OM!

Touch the ground with your hands and see all of the negative energies that you have banished with the white light flow into the earth. Offer a prayer to help heal yourself and to help heal all those who suffer in the world. Sit and breathe deeply for a moment. You are done!

People who have done this simple exercise have felt remarkable results. Some just feel refreshed and reenergized; others feel things inside them shift or change dramatically. You may actually expel physical toxins and problems when you next visit the restroom! Try this several times and you may be surprised at how much better your body, mind, and spirit feel! You may also do this for others.

Remember, your body *is* the temple of the divine and it is the dwelling place of your Guardian Angel. It is the hardware necessary for the software your Guardian Angel will download! Purify it, keep it in good working order, tend it and keep it balanced. You will not only have a better life and attitude, you will automatically bring yourself closer to your Guardian Angel! Remember: *Your Guardian Angel knows you better than any other being and exists for only one reason—to guide, help, and comfort you so that you can follow your path.*

Chapter 5:

Expanding Your Relationship
with Your Guardian Angel

Once you have established communication with your Guardian Angel and are working to nurture your awareness of it on a daily basis, that relationship, like any other, must be built upon. When you begin to perceive what your angel is saying and to get clear and regular guidance from it, you can expand the scope of your life and of your interactions with the world. It is like finding a particular radio frequency. Your angel is always "broadcasting," even if the signal is only picked up occasionally and often with great interference.

Once you have tuned in to your angel's signal, you have to turn up the volume so that it can respond directly to you in positive ways. When you are confident in your ability to receive regular messages from your personal angel, you can establish a significant back-and-forth communication with the divine on a very real and practical level. You don't have to simply hope or wish for guidance and inspiration; you can be sure of it.

There are three basic strategies you can use to fine-tune this communication. You can strengthen the already-established bond by continuing the exercises described in the previous chapters. You can broaden the field of interaction by providing new specific modes of communication that both you and your angel can understand and utilize. And you can expand communication with your angel through creativity. Engaging and playing with the creative process can provide a nonintellectual means of communication and expression between you and your Guardian Angel.

STRENGTHENING THE BOND

Once you have established a connection with and awareness of your Guardian Angel, you must work to strengthen this bond so your angel can communicate with you and inspire you and bring creative joy to your life. Once the pattern of your Guardian Angel is clear to your eyes and other senses, both outer and inner, you can never lose sight of this divine helper.

You are now faced with a choice: Are you happy with your present relationship with your Guardian Angel, knowing it is there and calling upon it in times of need?

Or do you wish a closer union and deeper communication? If you are pleased with what you have accomplished so far and it is enough for you, feel free to stop reading here and move on with your life! If you wish to go further, read on. Nothing is forcing you; God has given you the True Will to evolve and move forward in your life as much or as little as you want. The choice is ultimately up to you and your own Will. Your Guardian Angel only wants what is best for you and will settle for whatever relationship you wish. But do not be surprised if, like a loving parent, your angel gently urges you to become the best you can be! That is its purpose, after all.

To strengthen your initial bond with your Guardian Angel, you must extend it further outward into your life and further inward into the depths of your being. Throughout history there have been hidden societies of people who have accomplished this great work of uniting with the Guardian Angel and who have preserved the knowledge of the process down through the ages. They have appeared within every religion and tradition, often as mystics or visionaries. Over the centuries, they have used symbols to teach this process. Let's begin this chapter by examining one classic and persistent symbol of the Guardian Angel and the process of union with the divine and see how it relates to the practical steps you can take to further strengthen your bond with your own angel.

THE POWERS OF THE SPHINX

The sphinx has represented the ultimate riddle or mystery for several thousand years and persists as a symbol of hidden wisdom in many traditions. A sphinx is a mythical creature with the head of a man and the body of an animal, often a lion. The giant Sphinx at Giza in Egypt is the most famous example, but there are many others. In hidden traditions passed down in Western spiritual circles, the sphinx is used to explain how you can grow closer to your Guardian Angel by training your mind and body to adjust and focus in such a way as to receive the transmissions of the Guardian Angel. The powers of the sphinx are the keys to this process. Let's pull away the veils of mystical symbolism that surround this creature and plainly reveal what the mysteries mean for you and your Guardian Angel.

Traditionally, the "riddle of the sphinx" is a puzzle that the Hero (you!) must unravel. The riddle, as reported in Greek myth, is this: What has four legs in the morning, two at midday, and three at sunset? The answer? Man. Man crawls on all fours as a child, walks upright as an adult, and hobbles on three legs (with a cane) in old age. This riddle symbolizes the passage of time and the process of transformation that every human being experiences. Yet the sphinx itself is removed from this cycle of birth and death. How can this be so?

The sphinx is often shown with wings outstretched, and can be either male or female in form. In fact, as we will see, the sphinx is your Guardian Angel, the being who is and yet is not you, who personifies the higher aspect of your animal being—

your body and senses governed and controlled by your mind. The wings symbolize the divine harmony of body and mind—a harmony that is eternal in nature. As you age and transform, your Guardian Angel watches. It can seem impassive and distant, but once you have solved the riddle it poses, you have a firm ally forever.

The sphinx has four legendary powers: *to know, to will, to dare,* and *to keep silent.* Together, these four powers culminate in a fifth: *the power of the spirit to connect with the divine.* These powers are modes of behavior you can adopt that will inevitably lead you to a closer embrace with your Guardian Angel.

The Power to Know

There are two types of knowledge—internal and external. Both need to be expanded if you want to draw closer to your Guardian Angel.

Many assume that learning about things and storing that learning as knowledge is a passive process. You watch a movie or read a book about something and then you "know" about it. Nothing could be further from the truth. Knowing is an active sport! You must *seek* knowledge of something for it to be acquired and taken into your mind, both consciously and unconsciously. Perhaps you seek knowledge of gardening because you have bought a house with beds of flowers. First, you ask friends about gardening, then you read a book or do some research on the Internet, and finally you get to it and get your hands dirty. As you garden, you make errors and correct them with more information. You find that some of the advice you gathered, some of the information, is very helpful and right for your garden. Other information is either useless or wrong. Some things you read simply don't apply to your garden and some of the advice people give you won't work for your garden. Over time, you learn what works and what doesn't, what information is right for you and what isn't, and you build on that knowledge with your own experience. In fact, your knowledge becomes internalized. It becomes *intuitive.* The gathering of information, the discovery of what is right for you, the elimination of useless information, all of this can only come through experience, through direct interaction with the information. At this point, it becomes *part* of you. This is real knowledge.

This kind of information-in-action is what I mean by the sphinx's power to know. Through the ongoing interaction between your body/material world and your mind/intellectual world a union develops, a deep understanding of what is right and what is not in furthering your goals and Will in *your* reality. Your garden is different from everyone else's garden, just as your life, your reality, your mind and body are all different from everyone else's. Thus information, while necessary, is simply food for the mind. If not internalized, if not given over to your Higher Self, it is mere dross.

To know something is to encounter it, grasp it, and internalize it so that it becomes part of your worldview. The simple act of knowing is a deep proposition that most people take for granted. In order to become closer to your Guardian Angel, you must fully take upon yourself the power of knowing.

How can you accomplish this? Separate in your mind, clearly, those things you really know from those things you think are true because you read about them, saw them on the news, or were told about them. If you have not interacted with the facts on a personal level, then you do not know them. To know something is to become part of it, consciously and unconsciously. Some call this belief, but belief can occur without foundation. In fact, some would define faith as just this: The ability to believe something without sure knowledge of it.

So, what do I know? I know my wife and son love me. I know that certain plants will almost always grow well in my garden. I know when a student in my class does not understand something. I know how to cook a number of dishes. I know how to greet people in Japan, Nepal, Indonesia, and other countries. And I know many other things. I know these things with a certainty, to the point where they are simply extensions of my being, not beliefs or opinions that may change on a whim.

Your head is full of "stuff." Most of it comes from other people and from sources over which you have little control and that have very little to do with you. This "stuff," for the most part, is junk. It hinders your communion with your Guardian Angel. You can derive great power from merely pushing these piles of ideas, opinions, and bits of information into the garbage and focusing on what you really know. In the place of true knowing (gnosis) resides the Guardian Angel.

Spend a few hours one night just sitting quietly and contemplating this one question: *What do I really know?* You may want to write down some of your answers. Very soon you will realize that the things you know are the things you do not have to think about. This is the source of the great power of knowing. Your ego constantly latches onto anything that makes it bigger or grander. These things make you feel better or more righteous, whether they are real or not. Those things you really know are not accepted and pulled deep into your being by your ego; they are absorbed into your being by your Guardian Angel. It is only through your Guardian Angel that you can truly know something so thoroughly that you do not question it. This kind of knowing is like breathing; it is natural and instinctive and spiritual.

Now, there is a caution here. Don't assume that because you feel something is true that you truly know it. You must verify this deep knowledge over and over. Your ego will quickly get hip to this process and try to convince you that you know things that are beneficial to you or that make you feel good! Test, verify, make these known things part of your active life. If they were not true, let them go.

The point is this: You must develop the power to know. Knowledge is where your body and mind meet in spirit; it is internal and external in nature. The things you know and the power you have to know cuts through all falsehood, lies, propaganda, silliness, and useless information like a knife, revealing the core truths that underlie all things. You can only know some things, yet these form the foundation of your being. By being clear about what makes up that foundation, you avoid being pulled this way and that by others who want to use you, convert you, brainwash you, or get you to do what *they* want you to do. True knowledge empowers you to hold fast to your Will.

THE POWER TO WILL

Let's take a moment to define the word "will." Someone who is willful is simply stubborn or determined. In terms of personal power, however, I use the term "will" in a different way. To differentiate it from its common usage, I call it True Will. Your True Will is the path you were born to take in this life. It is what you were meant to do on this planet, in this life. It is the orbit of your star, if you like. You can see what this means in the real world by simply observing people who have excelled at something, people who knew early in life: YES! This is what I am here for!

Think of Picasso or Einstein or Bach or Tiger Woods! All these people, through some sort of inner guidance, somehow found what it was they were supposed to do in life and did it to the best of their ability. Some call this being in the groove. Well, that groove is called True Will.

Everyone has a True Will. It is determined by many things, and different traditions characterize it differently. We need not accept or reject any of these beliefs to recognize the reality of True Will. We need only accept that the goal of your Guardian Angel is to help you accomplish *your* True Will.

What is your True Will? Ask yourself these questions and really think about the answers:

What do I do that really makes me happy?

What do I do that really fills me with a feeling of accomplishment and satisfaction?

When do I complain about not having enough free time or fantasize about doing something else?

What is it I want to do? What would I really like to do, if only I could?

What have I tried in life that instantly felt right?

Now, go back and mentally cross off all the things you want to do, but that do not fill you with a feeling of being just right for you. For example, I love skiing, but I don't feel a deep inner satisfaction when I ski! I just like it! Same with hiking and swimming. I therefore know that it is not my True Will to be an Olympic swimmer or to climb Mount Everest! Yet I have been a teacher for eighteen years, have left the profession several times for better paying jobs with more prestige, then returned to teaching. And each time I returned to teaching, it was like coming home. It felt like a glove that just fit me. I knew that this was my calling, whether I liked it all the time or not.

It is very likely that, upon reflection, you will get some glimmer of what your True Will is. It may or may not have anything to do with what you are doing or how your life is going at the moment! If this is the case, you are very likely unhappy. It is that simple.

Think of your Guardian Angel as the personification or "mask" of your True Will. Your True Will is the essential core or path of your being from birth to death;

thus your Guardian Angel strives from the moment of your birth to keep your feet on the right path or way. Remember the classic picture of a Guardian Angel hovering over a child, protecting it and keeping it on the safe path through the dangerous woods? This path is the way you are supposed to go through life; it is your True Will. As it unfolds, you will accomplish those things you were meant to do, help those you were meant to help, and evolve mentally, physically, and spiritually in ways that you are meant to evolve.

No one can tell you what that path is; no one can help you find it and keep to it. No one, that is, except your Guardian Angel, who not only intimately knows every twist and turn of this path you are to take, but is in fact the very essence of this path! A connection with your angel thus makes you more aware of your path and able to follow your own unique True Will. Unfortunately, this message has often been misunderstood by some as an opportunity to simply sign over the responsibility for their lives to a particular prophet or religious teacher. They mistakenly think, by following another, they can follow their own way. Remember: Your True Will is unique!

Quietly meditating on this proves that it is simply wrong to follow another when God has clearly placed you on this planet to do something unique as part of a greater pattern. If we were all meant to go the same way, we would all look and feel the same, yet it is clear that every single child is unique. Does it not follow then that we all have our own paths or ways to go in this world? If there is a larger pattern to the great life, doesn't it make sense that we are each a unique part of this pattern and that the way we live our lives and affect the world is part and parcel of that unique way?

In Eastern philosophy, all is seen in terms of *yin* and *yang*, roughly positive and negative (though light and shadow are better translations). All things are said to be part of the origin of yin and yang. This origin of all things, beyond conception, the ultimate source of all, is called the *Tao*. Although many people have heard of Tao, fewer know about its compliment, called *Teh*. Tao is the limitless source of all things and is beyond all thought or conception (God); Teh is how the Tao works itself out in this world. Teh is True Will, for the way that Tao or God works itself out in this "world of ten thousand things" is very much through mankind. Just as everything on the planet is created of a mixture of yin and yang, so too is every person. How every person, including you, flows through life is determined by their Teh.

This tells us something important about True Will: If you try to sail against the tide, if you act against your inner nature or True Will, your life becomes filled with chaos and unpleasantness because you are going against the grain. When you try to be someone you are not, the universe ceases to help you and seems to hinder you at every turn! Yet when you sail with the wind, with the tide, along the path you are meant to be on, things fall into place. The universe is behind you and speeds you on your way.

We have all had days where nothing went right and the universe seemed against us. Extend this idea. Have you ever taken a job that you knew was wrong for you? Even though others in that job were perfectly happy and productive, you were not happy and things seemed to go against you all the time? Have you had relationships like this as well? There is a simple answer that, in your heart, you know is true: These situations were not right for you! Your ego wants to label these experiences bad or negative, but the reality is much simpler. They may have been right for others, but not for you. They were *not part of your True Will*.

Exercise 11: Seeing Your True Will

Sit quietly and close your eyes. See yourself as a blazing star in space, slowly moving in your own specific orbit. Look back and see where you have been in your life. See the successful moments, accomplishments, and relationships as points along your orbital path. See all the "wrong" moments—failed relationships, bad jobs, and "fish out of water" experiences—as moments that pulled you off the orbit you made through space. Think carefully. What do the on-track experiences and relationships have in common? What sorts of things got you off track and made you unhappy?

Where are you now in this vision? Are you right on track with your orbit? Slightly off? Way off? Project this orbit into the future from the perspective of past positive experiences you had. Where should your orbit take you? Is this where you are headed? If not, what can you do to get back on track?

No one can tell you where you have been or where you are meant to go. All I can tell you is this, and I know it for certain: Every man and every woman is a star. Each star has an optimal orbit that it needs to follow to be all that it can be, to make the most of this life and to fulfill part of the larger divine pattern. Many forces around you, including other people, institutions, and negative traditions, may try their best, for their own reasons, to pull your star out of orbit, to snare it and enslave it to another Will. It is the duty of every star to resist these forces and to persist in seeking real happiness by doing its own True Will— that is, following the proper path, regardless of what others say or do. Is this the easy way? No, of course not. But it is the way of personal power. And you have a great ally in this work—your Guardian Angel.

The primary reality check you have to keep you aligned with your True Will is your Guardian Angel, because your angel personifies your True Will. Whenever you are unsure of a decision or path that you deep down *know* is right, but on which others may cast doubt, this is the time to seek the guidance and inspiration of your angel. It will always let you know in some way whether you are on the right track or not, by both external and internal means. I have found myself suddenly fired or pushed out of several jobs that, looking back, were all wrong for me. I had taken them because I thought (!) I should or because I was convinced by others that I should, even though I was uneasy from the start—a sure sign!

I currently have a teaching position that pays less than my previous job, yet it gives me time to write and supplies a lot of personal support. Although I was told by others it was a foolish choice, I now go to work every day knowing that this is right for me. I don't have a perfect day every day—there are always problems—but the gnawing uncertainty and deep-seated unease I felt previously is gone completely. This job may not last forever or even be the thing I am meant to do for the next ten years, but for now, I know it is my True Will.

Remember, it is *now* that matters most. Your ego (and others) will try to convince you that you can do what you need to do later, that you can put off doing your True Will until you have accomplished one thing or another. In some cases, this may be true, but many people who took a job or started a friendship or moved to another town at the behest of others "just for a little while," have found themselves stuck in that place a decade later, still dissatisfied.

I am convinced that most people who are basically unhappy, who are mean or unkind, who self-medicate with food, alcohol, or drugs (prescribed or illegal) are miserable because they are not doing their True Wills. These people have been convinced by society and the people around them that they need to do this or that, that this is the way to live, and that they should therefore be happy. They are not, and therefore assume that something is wrong with them. They try to fill up the emptiness with more food, more sex, more drugs, more something. These people simply need to find and follow their True Wills.

The solution is to think deeply about what it is you should be doing with your life (your Guardian Angel is giving you hints all the time) *and do it!* You are not on this Earth to do what others want or expect you to do. You are here to do one thing: your True Will. Do that and the oceans will part for you. The way will become clear and you will not only be happier, you will help everyone around you be a better person, both by the positive energy you emanate and by example. You will also find yourself walking in step with your Guardian Angel, because your angel is always following your True Will, whether you are or not! Thus the path of True Will is key to becoming closer to your Guardian Angel!

THE POWER TO DARE

To dare means to do something you know is right despite danger or fear. The word hints at courage or bravery, but is more subtle. To dare means to take a risk. Why is this such an important power to have when pursuing spiritual development and becoming closer to your Guardian Angel? Because to know something and to Will something are useless if you do not *dare to do it.* It is important to be clear on what you know; it is even more important to figure out what your Will is. But the hardest part is to take both of these powers and put them into practice by daring to do what you need to do.

It is not always the big decisions and choices that are the most important; often it is the little ones. Those little decisions can be the ones that, in the long run, lead to bigger decisions. They are also the ones that are easily imposed or pushed by others or by society. If you are haunted by a number of "if only I had…" or "I should have…" feelings, look back at your life. What things did you not do that you wanted to do? What things do you regret doing? Some of these regrets may have seemed small at the time—like choosing to take up the flute instead of the piano at school because a parent wanted you to do so. But what were the results? Make a mental list of some of these regrets and follow the threads of them to the present. What experiences or situations do you *not* have in your life now because you did not do those things you initially felt impelled to do? This feeling of impulsion, as you realize by now, may have been a sign that your Guardian Angel was attempting to guide you.

The things you truly regret not doing or the choices you truly regret making all have a root cause: You did not dare to do what you knew deep down was the right thing for you to do. Maybe you were convinced or pushed or advised or bullied into that choice. Maybe you simply did not want to deal with the opposition you knew you'd encounter by choosing that path. In any event, one thing should be clear from this reflection: The power of daring to do what you know you should do because it is part of your Will is a crucial power in spiritual evolution and in connecting with your Guardian Angel.

Why? Because as you become closer to your Guardian Angel, it will begin to communicate with you through your outer reality and through your inner mind. Much of what your angel will communicate to you is guidance and help. This guidance and help will come in very practical and real terms, and it will almost certainly change aspects of your life, including job, living situation, relationships, and emotional sharing. Change of any sort is hard, sometimes painful. The people around you often have their own ideas about what you should and should not do. They often have problems with the shifts you will be compelled to make. I cannot tell you what those shifts will be; no one can! But they will lead to positive, life-affirming decisions and changes as the divine is brought into your life, as your Guardian Angel shows you what you need to be doing in this life, what your path really is.

One student of mine desperately wanted to be a graphic artist, but her parents convinced her it was useless and pushed her into a business career. She was basically unhappy with her life for decades. She came to a Guardian Angel workshop and, during an exercise, her angel came to her and told her to do art! After denying she had any talent, as her parents had told her, she dared to try drawing. A few months later she quit her lucrative job and became a graphic artist. Last I heard from her, she had found financial success and was happier than she had ever been.

It is one thing to know what you will to do, but can you actually do it? What if society frowns on it? What if your loved ones do not want you to do it? What if people think you are crazy or are having a midlife crisis? Will you dare to make such changes in your life? If not, your Guardian Angel cannot help you. In fact, no one can help you. No one can improve you but you. No one knows your True Will but you.

And it is *never* too late! No matter how long you have put it off, you can still learn to play the piano, lose fifty pounds, start a new career, help the homeless, visit Africa, stop smoking, or do whatever it is that you know it is your Will to do! All you need is a little courage to defend your choices, and for that you can call upon your Guardian Angel at any time or place.

Your Guardian Angel is your guide and your support, your teacher and your arm to lean on. When you dare to take that leap of faith, know that your Guardian Angel is right there with you, even if others are not.

The Power to Be Silent

Think about the last time someone tried to pick an argument with you, or was loud and hostile to you, but you simply stood your ground and remained silent. What happened? Likely they backed down or simply went away after a while—a fire with no fuel soon burns out. When people are fighting, no matter who starts it, it takes both of them to keep it going. Silence can indeed be golden.

When you are talking, you are not listening. When you are quiet but thinking about other things—that is, inner noise and chatter—you are not listening. When you are quiet, both internally and externally, truly quiet, you can truly listen to another voice. That voice may be coming from a friend or loved one. It may also be coming from your Guardian Angel.

Try sitting for ten minutes or longer and being silent—completely quiet, no speaking or humming at all. The first thing you discover, as anyone who meditates also discovers, is that the minute you are quiet, your inner mind begins to try to fill the void. Old pop songs, grocery lists, memories of the last movie you saw, almost anything is apt to pop up. Rather than try to hold back this inner ego-chatter, just let it go through you. Don't attach anything to this mental chatter. Eventually, this inner noise will die down. With a little practice and a bit of patience, you will reach a place of silence where you can be very quiet, very still.

This quiet time opens a door. You can really hear the world about you, the whisper of a friend or loved one, and also the inner quiet voice of your Guardian Angel. This is why, no matter what your religion or faith, periods of quiet contemplation or meditation are so very important. It is only when the agitation around you stops that the waters of your inner mind can settle and truth can be seen. This can only be done through silence.

Silence creates a zone of peace around you. An angry or aggressive person who is met with calm silence will usually seek elsewhere for someone to fight. Silence opens your mind to reality and time seems to slow down. The pause you take in the constant input/output of noise and words literally recharges your batteries and renews your spirit. It also puts a gag on your ego, which flits from desire to reaction to stimulus without real thought. It lets you detach and not get snared by every stimulus that passes by. Only in silence can you find your true center, and only in this true center can you connect with your Guardian Angel.

Try this simple exercise. For ten minutes every day, simply be silent. It can be in your car, before you go to sleep, as you wake up, or maybe over that first cup of coffee. Just be silent. Don't do anything. Don't think about or visualize anything. Just *be*. After a few days, you may want to record the results of this silent time in your journal. You will be surprised how important that quiet time may become.

Learn to be silent actively. Why do you need to reply to everyone who speaks to you? Why feel compelled to fill in gaps in conversations? In Western cultures, silence is seen as awkward or unnatural. We hurry to fill these silences with idle chatter for no real reason. Try cultivating silence as a way of communicating.

Sit quietly with a loved one for periods of time. Do not feel compelled to chat about anything! The silence can be rich and powerful, loving and special. When someone is being antagonistic, rude, or overbearing, simply refuse to respond. Be silent. Let the negativity flow around you. If they push you to reply, simply state that you have nothing to say. Or say nothing! Realize this: It is OK to be quiet!

At first, this will be uncomfortable. You have been convinced all your life that silence is rude or strange, yet many cultures consider silence companionable, friendly, and natural! Silence opens your heart, your mind, and your inner being. It lets your ego rest so your true self, your Guardian Angel, can shine forth. This is why Christian, Hindu, Buddhist, and Moslem holy men and women have been taking vows of silence for centuries. In silence, there is contemplation of that which is beyond the material world. Inner patterns, consciousness, and outer awareness are sharpened and brought to the fore. This process, of course, will bring you closer to your Guardian Angel and to the divine of which it is an expression.

There is a final and most powerful use of silence. This is called empowerment or transmission or blessing. Christians call this the descent of the Holy Spirit; Hindus call it *Shakti pat* or divine energy blessing. It is simply this: The transfer of a blessing of energy directly from a spiritual teacher, priest, reverend, or guru to a student, worshipper, or *chela*. This is done by a laying on of hands, by sprinkling water, or simply by the direction of energy or *Shakti* from one person to another. The key to the effectiveness of this process is that it be done in silence. The one who is receiving the energy must be open, silent, and completely receptive mentally, physically, and spiritually.

This book recognizes the power and effectiveness of all spiritual teachers, thus the blessings you seek are up to you and will follow in accord with the True Will with which God blessed you at birth. Yet the core teaching of this book is this: The greatest and most perfect spiritual teacher you can ever have is the one that God gave you at birth, your Guardian Angel. Your Guardian Angel often will set up special times and moments and experiences for you. These important learning or transformation points in your life will only truly be effective and filled with gnosis or inner knowledge of the divine if you are truly receptive to them. When one of those moments or experiences occurs, you will know it. At that time, be silent. Let the silence open your inner self to the depths and power of this divine blessing. Let the Shakti or energy that your

Guardian Angel has led you to, flow into you and through you. You will never be the same; you will be a better person. This is why your Guardian Angel exists: To help and empower you. Receive this gift in silence.

THE POWER OF THE SPIRIT IS TO CONNECT WITH THE DIVINE

Joined together, these four powers of the sphinx yield a power that is greater than the sum of its parts. The power to know, to will, to dare, and to be silent result in a union with the Guardian Angel that is subtle, long-term, and amazingly strong. The growth of spiritual insight is gradual. By simply coordinating the constant cultivation of the sphinx's four powers, you inadvertently develop a fifth. This fifth element is veiled in many different symbols and analogies, but comes down in the end to this simple truth: Your goal is to move yourself into the place where your Guardian Angel already resides/exists and join yourself with the divine. The powers of the sphinx, cultivated over time, will help you achieve this. *Thus the riddle of the sphinx is solved (you are your Guardian Angel!) and the human and animal are united and transcended by the wings of spirit.*

EXPANDING COMMUNICATION WITH YOUR GUARDIAN ANGEL

As you get closer to your Guardian Angel, it becomes closer to you, just as two people who become better and better friends can communicate more easily with each other as they get closer. Over time, your angel will be able to communicate directly with you through an inner voice and through your ability to simply know things it wants you to know. It will also communicate through coincidences. But you can develop other means that your angel can use to talk to you as well.

When your Guardian Angel communicates, it is in a language that is far above normal one-dimensional human communication. Angels are a higher order of being; they communicate in several different dimensions at once, on levels of perception and comprehension that we can only dream about. So if your Guardian Angel is speaking to you on a level far above what you can possibly comprehend, how can you translate its messages?

For the answer to this, look to your own world. How do two people who do not speak the same language communicate? Through a third language that bridges the gulf between the two. This medium of communication must be flexible and must be common to both people. Sign language, body language, a lingua franca or trade language like Swahili in Africa—all are used to help people find a common tongue.

The forms of communication that you have available to you for commerce with your guardian angel are a bit unusual due to the spiritual nature of angels! This chapter focuses on three basic mediums of communication that you and your Guardian Angel can use with increasing fluency as you converse with each other. While you may doubt that such communication is possible, these forms have been used for centuries to facilitate communication between Guardian Angels and humans. As your bond with your Guardian Angel grows stronger, it may reveal other means of communication not discussed here. Remember: the final word on such things lies with your angel, not with any book or other authority. God has directed your angel to guide and help you in the best ways possible. Some of the modes of communication I present here can help immensely. Yet you may be uncomfortable with one or more of them, and that is fine. Your Guardian Angel will let you know what is right for you!

Your Guardian Angel converses with your conscious mind and ego through your unconscious mind. I can't help but think of human researchers teaching sign language to gorillas in order to communicate with them. Our Guardian Angels must sometimes feel the same frustrations at only being able to communicate with us through such a narrow spectrum of language! Angels can often communicate with humans through almost any symbols and feelings. These can take many forms, including dreams, oracles, augury, tarot, runes, and numerology. This chapter will now discuss modes and means of communication that bypass the normal, rational, ego-controlled methods. The language of the spirit and of the Guardian Angel may not make rational sense in this limited and material world, but you must bridge the gap between those two different worlds!

How can you comprehend an angel's mind or point of view? You cannot. The best you can do is try a variety of ways of communicating and see which method or mode your Guardian Angel prefers. By doing so, you open a door for your angel to reach down from its exalted state of being into the realm of matter and causality and give you direct guidance. As long as you are open to this, it will happen.

DREAMS

In most religions, dreams are seen as a way of communicating with the divine and, more important, as a way for the divine to communicate with us. From the dream of Jacob's Ladder in the Bible to the famous Zen story of a man dreaming he is a butterfly, (or was it the other way around?!), dreams have been used throughout human history as evidence of divine consciousness. In Asia, shrines and temples are often built to divine dreams. A number of churches in Europe have been inspired by dreams as well.

The dream realm is the "middle ground"of the divine. Carl Jung noticed that his patients encountered powerful symbolic images and beings in their dreams that were trying to help them find healing and peace. This process of inner spiritual growth was not evident in all dreams, but only in very special "true" dreams that were often in color and often impressed themselves deeply upon the minds of the dreamers.

Why would the unconscious mind create such powerful images and enact such complex inner dramas? Jung felt that all the myths, legends, rituals, and religious experiences in true dreams provided a means for dealing with the Self, bringing inner peace, unity, and the wholeness called individuation. The goal of this process is to bring your conscious mind into contact with your Guardian Angel, what Jung called the Self. To discover more about this, Jung turned increasingly to the study of dreams.

Ah, but what does this have to do with you? Simply this: From the moment you make an effort to join with your Guardian Angel, it will be trying its hardest to surmount the communicative obstacles between you. Like an ocean pounding at a wall, your angel will try in every way it can to communicate with you and help you. That is, after all, its job!

When you begin to make any serious effort to open up to the guidance and help your angel has to offer you, your dreams will change. Earlier, I suggested that you keep a journal of your work with your Guardian Angel. I also strongly suggest that you keep a journal of your dreams. As you open to your Guardian Angel, you will notice three types of dreams that suddenly begin to occur, aside from your normal dreams that come and go through your sleeping hours.

The first, precognition dreams, are rare, but they do happen. These dreams show something real happening in the future. Your Guardian Angel may send these to you to warn you, or help you avert a problem, or to simply affirm a choice. I'll never forget my first sight of the university where I was to do my master's work. I had seen it in a dream! I knew then and there that I was doing what I was supposed to be doing. It was a nice reality check from my Guardian Angel!

Precognition dreams are rare, but specific. Yet if you don't remember them or if you do not heed them, they are not helpful! Keeping a journal helps in many ways. First, you will often forget dreams if you do not write them down right after waking. Second, they give you written proof that you are not crazy, that you really had that dream and it really did happen!

The second type of dream is the symbolic dream that seeks to communicate something important or that seeks to teach you something. I call these "lesson" dreams. These dreams can take some time to unravel, because they communicate in a roundabout way with symbols and feelings that make perfect sense in the dream, but that can be hard to untangle back in the waking world! They are often in vivid color and are hard to forget. You will know your Guardian Angel when it appears in these and other dreams. It will appear as a figure of great power or importance, often as an elderly teacher or sage. Jung also notes that the Self (Guardian Angel) can sometimes appear simply as a disembodied voice of great power!

Once, my Guardian Angel appeared as a guru in a complex dream with many symbols. This figure walked me through a library until it came to a special book that it pulled down and showed to me. It had my name on it! My Guardian Angel then proceeded to explain this book and show the many strange symbols and images in it. I could not understand most of what happened, as is usual in this sort of dream, but I awoke with the knowledge that I was to be an author, something I'd never done or planned to do in my life! Five books later, here I am!

I've had deep and powerful dreams like this about death, about making decisions that affected my life, about dealing with anger and about how to be a better person.

Sometimes I'm the hero of the dream and I have to go to hell and back, or fight monsters, or embrace the shadow side of myself. What separates these from other run-of-the-mill adventure dreams is that there is always a kind of summary or moral lesson at the end. Often, the action is interrupted by moments of awareness or *waking inside the dream*. Once I had a dream of flying in which I awoke in the dream and was able to control the flying. The voice of my Guardian Angel boomed out in the dream that all children can do this—leave their bodies—that it is natural but that at a certain age they are taught that it is impossible and so lose the gift!

Many of the teachings or lessons you receive in this way will, of course, be just for you. These lesson dreams will help you come to terms with personal pain, anger, loss, and inner turmoil. Most often, they serve to comfort and teach, to let you know that all is well, to show you how to let go of pain and turn toward love.

The third type of dream is the experience dream. I call these dreams "initiation dreams" because the experience itself *is* the message. You awake from initiation dreams a changed person. These dreams are direct empowerments from your Guardian Angel that serve to enlighten you. Throughout history, great figures like Alexander the Great, Napoleon, Joan of Arc, and Winston Churchill have awakened from great and pivotal dreams having experienced something that changed them and showed them the paths they were meant to take to fulfill their destinies—the True Will that the divine had set for them in life.

I have had only a handful of initiation dreams, but I remember one quite clearly. I was questioning my job, my place in the world, what I was doing—in short, I was questioning everything, especially what possible good I could do in the world. In a dream, I saw a spiritual teacher I knew, yet I knew that he represented something more. He was naked and glowing with a powerful light. He took me through an experience that transformed me, leading me through a maze that was the world and that somehow revealed the essence of the world through symbols and images. What I remember most clearly is a prison he showed me framed with a huge metal gate made of bars and locks. Behind those bars were millions of miserable, impoverished people in rags. They were depressed, listless, completely numb, and despondent. He pointed to the bars and showed me how to throw my energy at them. Didn't I want to free these miserable people? I threw all my energy at the bars with the yell of some special word of power he taught me. Suddenly the bars exploded and all the people were free! They ran out of the jail, happily yelling and dancing. My Guardian Angel then turned to me and, without words, told me this: Go free the prisoners.

I awoke a different person. I know that my job, whatever it may be, is to help "free the prisoners." Thus, I am a teacher and writer, because part of the lesson I was taught is that many people are prisoners of their own minds, their own limitations and negative beliefs. People are often more creative and wonderful than they think they are. I can do things to help people see this.

The more you write down your dreams, the easier it will be to remember them.

Once your Guardian Angel knows that you are paying attention, it will open up the gates of dreamland ever wider to your view. Your dreams will have more meaning and you will be readying yourself for those dreams that are important, those that contain the truths your Guardian Angel wants you to receive.

Don't forget, however, that dreams are just dreams. They can be significant and powerful; they can reveal important truths and communicate key bits of knowledge that help you grow, but they are dreams. You can dream of a great feast yet awaken hungry. The point is that while dreams may communicate important things, it is what you *do* with that knowledge in the real world that is most important.

ORACLES

Oracles show the will of the divine through the seemingly chance appearance of symbols, patterns of sticks, bones, or cards, or through other apparently random patterns. These patterns are interpreted by the person asking the question or by a seer. Using an oracle for divine guidance or inspiration is very different from going to a fortune-teller and having your fortune read, however. Oracles allow you to communicate with the unseen, to get specific advice and other communications from a specific divine being. Your Guardian Angel may use oracles as a means to communicate with you through apparent coincidences.

Many people of different religions use oracles to help them make decisions. Buddhists consult special oracles in temples or use the *I Ching*. Devout Christians open the Bible at random to search for an answer to a troubling question. Even if you feel uncomfortable with fortune-telling or psychic sciences, you can still use oracles to communicate with your Guardian Angel. In this sense, you are *not* seeking to know the future; you are only seeking communication from your Guardian Angel, your inner and direct link with God. Of course, if you are uncomfortable with any of these methods of oracular communication, do not use them. If you try one or more of them, you will soon find that your Guardian Angel prefers one mode of communication over another. Try and see.

What follows are very brief descriptions of oracles that have been used to communicate with Guardian Angels. No one is better than another; the choice is completely up to you—and, of course, your angel. There are other types of oracles not mentioned here. Some are very complex; some are oriented to a specific culture. In fact, there is no limit to what you can use as a medium for communication between you and your Guardian Angel. I know of several people who created their own symbolic systems to use for communication or adapted existing systems as their Guardian Angels instructed them. A simple search of your local bookstore will show you all sorts of decks and oracles and systems that you can use. Often simply asking your angel to recommend something will draw you to the right tool, sometimes quite unexpectedly! Remember, your Guardian Angel knows you better than you know yourself and simply wants to help you in every way possible. As always, the choices are up to you and your angel. Trust your angel; open yourself to it. Ask and it shall be provided!

Bibliomancy is a very simple form of oracle that can be practiced anytime anywhere. All you need is a clear mind and a book. People often use the Bible or other holy books, but I have had great success using a dictionary or any book at hand!

Sit quietly with the book you have chosen. Close your eyes and surround yourself with white light, then call upon your Guardian Angel. When you are ready, silently ask your question. Keep it simple! When you are clear about the question and feel the touch of your Guardian Angel, turn the book around and around in your hands, keeping your eyes closed, then suddenly open it at random and stab your finger to a page. Open your eyes and read the word or phrase that you are pointing to. That is your answer!

Yes/No oracles have been used in Chinese temples and other places of worship for centuries to give simple negative or affirmative answers. Here is an example. You will need two coins that are the same or two small flat stones that clearly have "heads and tails" sides. Sit quietly, project white light about you, then contact your Guardian Angel and ask your yes/no question while holding the coins or stones in your cupped hands. When ready, drop the coins onto the table or floor in front of you. If they are both heads-up, the answer is a clear *yes*; if they are both tails-up, the answer is a clear *no*. If one is tails and the other is heads, the answer is *maybe* and the choice is completely yours. Or you can wait a while or restate the question and try again. Often an ambiguous response means that your question is too broad or your Guardian Angel is not sure what or how to answer.

Augury uses naturally occurring oracles that communicate divine will through the movements of birds and animals, or through the sudden appearance of objects or people. In a sense, your whole reality is one big oracle! The hardest part of auguries is discovering the symbolic meaning behind them, trying to comprehend what your Guardian Angel is saying to you. There is no set method for explaining auguries. Unfortunately, much will depend on what is stored in your mind, what has meaning for you, and what your Guardian Angel is trying to communicate. If this form of oracle interests you or your Guardian Angel indicates that is a good tool, you will need to build up an inner list of meanings as you go along. Many books of symbols also give meanings for various animals and plants.

Let me give an example. Let's say I am currently sitting with my laptop in my wooded backyard. To do an augury, I would sit quietly, surround myself with white light, and contact my Guardian Angel. Then I'd ask a question, or simply become open to any communication my angel wants to send me. I want to ask the question, "How can I best write this book?" Then I'd open my eyes and wait quietly until something caught my eye. It might be a bird (birds are the most common auguries) or an animal or, perhaps a special rock or flower or tree. For a moment that thing will take on special meaning for me, then will be gone. For me, here and now, I see a bee. This seems like a very good augury to me! As a bee, I must be industrious and I must gather information, insight, ideas, and inspiration from many flowers (sources), just as a bee gathers pollen. I also read the bee as a symbol of the Sun and of my Guardian Angel.

Those who draw great inspiration from the natural world will be drawn to auguries as a mode of communication with their Guardian Angels; others may not. One advantage of auguries is that you can practice them anytime and anywhere: driving to work, walking the dog, sitting in a park, even channel-surfing on TV! Augury is simply the practice of opening yourself to any sort of communication your Guardian Angel may want to give you using your reality as the medium! Be open, flexible, and clear and you will be surprised what your Guardian Angel will show you.

TRADITIONAL ORACLES

There are many traditional oracles you can use to communicate with your Guardian Angel. Again, the choice is up to you and your angel. If you are using a book to guide your questioning, ignore those parts that tell you about fortune-telling or telling the future. You will be using these methods in a different way. Learn what the various parts of the systems mean and what each stands for—but only in terms of communication in the present. Always keep in mind that your use of each oracle is specific, that the future is always flexible and is often up to you and your Will.

Feel free to use each oracle in ways not set out in the book or manual that comes with it. I find that simply analyzing one card from a tarot deck or one rune answers the question I have without the need for a more complex reading. I have also created my own ways of using oracles to communicate with my Guardian Angel. Sometimes I choose a card to represent my question, then pull another to represent my angel's answer.

Finally, if an oracle doesn't work for you or if it is uncomfortable for you to use, drop it! There are many others out there or you can make your own.

Tarot uses a special deck of that consists of twenty-two Major Arcana cards that roughly correspond to the archetypes or inner powers that Jung described, and fifty-six other cards that are essentially the same as the playing cards we use today. The Major Arcana cards are the more potent cards and some people use only them when asking their Guardian Angel questions. The remaining fifty-six cards are divided into four suits that correspond to the four elements: Coins represent earth and physical things; Swords represent fire, energy and power; Wands represent air, the mind, and intellectual things; Cups represent water and emotional matters. Most tarot decks come with books or manuals that give you good explanations of each card and its meaning.

Cartomancy uses a simple deck of playing cards as an oracle. Although similar to tarot, this is a very different system with different meanings ascribed to each card. There are a few books that give you information on this method, among them *Fortune Telling with Playing Cards* by Sophia. There are even a couple of decks that are specifically designed for oracle work. The one I use is called the *Sophia Deck*.

Runes originated thousands of years ago in Northern Europe as a very simple form of alphabet. The most common set of runes used today is called the *Futhark* runes, a set of around twenty-five symbols, depending on who is making the set. Most sets of runes come with a booklet that explains the meaning of each rune and how to cast the runes to tell fortunes. Runes can be remarkably effective in communication with your Guardian Angel. They have simple yet broad symbolic meanings, and are very primal in form and origin. I have found that those who clearly identify themselves as having Germanic, Scandinavian, or British roots are particularly comfortable with the runes and seem to use them more effectively in Guardian Angel communications than other oracles. Is there a genetic connection? This is something to discover for yourself!

I Ching is perhaps the oldest oracle in existence. Archeologists have discovered hexagrams (six-line images that make up the sixty-four patterns of the *I Ching*) in China that are over 4000 years old! This alone makes the *I Ching* worthy of respect. The *I Ching*, loosely translated as the "Book of Changes," is one of the most fascinating books and systems. The book itself is full of philosophy, poetry, advice, and truly amazing knowledge.

The *I Ching* operates on the assumption that everything in the world is a combination of yin and yang, and that anything in the world can be represented by one of sixty-four hexagrams composed of yin (open) and yang (closed) lines. There is far more to this system than I can possibly summarize here. It is a complex and interesting system full of meaning and rich with symbolism. I have been using the *I Ching* to communicate with my Guardian Angel for more than twenty-five years and it has been a powerful source of answers and advice. Though it takes some time to learn the system, once you have done so, it is a powerful tool.

NUMEROLOGY/GEMATRIA

Jung claimed that numbers are the most primal language. And, in fact, numbers are one form of communication that is not only universal but also seems to cross levels of consciousness and awareness. The simple binary code that lies behind a number of complex computer languages is a good example of this. Because numbers are so primal, they can be used to span the gulf between the infinite consciousness of your Guardian Angel and your own limited consciousness.

There are many books on the history of numbers, number theories, and number languages if this subject interests you. This book is primarily concerned with how numbers can help you attain practical communication with your Guardian Angel. In fact, numbers have proven to be an effective medium for such communication for thousands of years.

The central premise of number-system communication is that there are no chance encounters—that the universe, including everything around you, has meaning. Therefore, everything in your reality is a medium through which you can communicate with your Guardian Angel, and numbers can be used to convey that communication.

There are some very simple rules for using number systems to receive communications from your Guardian Angel. Your mind is like a computer. By downloading (remembering/using) a particular number system, you let your conscious and unconscious mind know that this is a new avenue of communication. Thus you need to *be consistent*. If you decide to use a system in which A = 1, then it must always equal 1. Do not change the attributes or components of the system or you will create an internal mess and sabotage your means of communication! No matter how silly or weird number systems seem, once you have chosen one, stick with it for at least six months. Give your mind time to really accept the program. Give your Guardian Angel time and space enough to begin to use it to communicate. Keep an open mind.

There are two different number systems that I have used over the years to communicate with my Guardian Angel. One is called *numerology*, which reduces everything to the digits 1-9 (or 10). In this system, each number corresponds to a simple energy or power or symbol. You can find this system in many books and on many websites.

The second type of system is based in the Qabalah, the ancient Hebrew system of numbers/meanings called *gematria*. In this system, numbers are traditionally ascribed to the Hebrew alphabet to discover the hidden mysteries in scripture like the Torah. It was later adapted by many non-Jewish mystics who used it to communicate and understand spiritual truths. Eventually, it was ascribed to English letters as well. Gematria takes numerology to a new level. In it, every letter is assigned a number:

A = 1	L = 30
B = 2	M = 40
G = 3	N = 50
D = 4	S = 60
H or E = 5	O = 70
V or W or U = 6	P = 80
Z = 7	X = 90
Ch = 8	Q = 100
T or Th = 9	R = 200
I or J or Y = 10	Sh = 300
K = 20	T = 400

This allows you to turn any word into a number. How does this help you communicate with your Guardian Angel? Simply by letting you change complex and unclear ideas and words into clear and subliminal numbers.

The idea behind gematria is that two words or ideas that equal the same number have the same root essence. Once a system like this has been accepted by your mind, patterns and meaningful numbers emerge from your everyday surroundings. You will be able to turn words into numbers, and numbers into words. This creates an unconscious symbolic interface that your Guardian Angel can and will use to communicate with and guide you.

For example, take the word "Sun." In gematria it equals the number 116 (60+6+50). Thus we can say that 116 is an important number, or at least that it has meaning that transcends its simple numerical value. Looking for other words that equal 116, we find the word "whole." This indicates an essential link between the two concepts. The words "Sun" and "whole" are thus linked in meaning and symbolic value. Why is this important? Because while I was driving home one night and thinking about this book and what a universal symbol of the Guardian Angel might be, I asked my Guardian Angel for a sign. Suddenly a yellow car passed with the license plate 116. I jotted it down and—lo and behold!—"Sun" and "whole"!

INTERACTING CREATIVELY WITH YOUR GUARDIAN ANGEL

A traditional saying claims that "an angel guides every act of creation." Creation and creativity, the making of something new and beautiful, imbued with meaning beyond what is obvious, is the heart and soul of the role of God in this world. In our limited human context, perhaps the word that best embodies this gift is "inspiration." Essentially, this is what you seek from your Guardian Angel and from God.

The word "inspiration" comes from the Latin *in spiritu*, meaning, "filled with spirit or divine power." So we can begin to widen our view of the spiritual to include all successful art! The awe, joy, intensity, and excitement you feel when you encounter a powerful and moving work of art is, in a sense, the touch of God and the awe of the divine. Because Van Gogh or Picasso did not create what many would characterize as religious art, it may surprise you to think of them in this way. Yet their paintings have brought much inspiration and divine awe to many admirers. Art, real art, shows you the hand of God, the movement of the spirit, the power and joy of creativity. It has the power to make you say "Ah!" as you are filled with a rush of impressions, emotions, and inspiration.

One of the traditional terms for the Guardian Angel is the Muse, that spirit of inspiration that visits every artist. No work of art exists that was not in some way inspired by the Guardian Angel of the artist who created it. Some people are born with talent—maybe a genetic predisposition to draw well or paint well or sculpt, compose music, play an instrument, dance or do some other art with inborn skill. The rest of us learn to do these things, knowing that we will never be geniuses like Bach or Van Gogh, but still finding pleasure in the act of creation. One thing is certain:

Everybody is creative, everybody can be inspired, and everybody can and should create art.

Someone once said that art is "food for the soul." In fact, your Guardian Angel thrives on the act of creation, and the bond between you and your angel will become stronger as you open yourself to inspiration and creativity. In short, your Guardian Angel lives to help you create beauty!

If God is everywhere, a vast matrix of life and awareness, then the apparent separateness of people, ideas, and art forms are all really illusion. If all is ever as it was and the divine is infinite and eternal, then it is merely the *aspects* of God that change, and this is what art is all about! A musician friend once said that "the dance of the Guardian Angel is in art." This it a core truth that points to a very simple, yet very powerful, means of bringing your Guardian Angel closer to you. To put it bluntly: Take in and produce as much art as possible!

Remember, you do not have to be a great artist to enjoy and get real emotional and spiritual pleasure from art. The creative part of you needs exercise, just as your body does. Ignore it and it will atrophy, like a limb that never gets used. Why is this part of you important? Because it is part and parcel of your soul and of the divine connection you have with God via your Guardian Angel. As a creature made in the image of the divine, you are *made* to create beauty. It is part of why you are here. Thus, the more you create, the closer you are to God.

Don't really know where to start in reenergizing your artistic, creative self? Looking for inspiration to get you started? Here are some practical suggestions:

- Think about the kinds of artistic, creative things you loved to do as a child. Maybe you loved various crafts, painting, drawing, playing an instrument, or some other artistic pursuit. Think deeply about it. Then go out and try to do it again! It is very likely that that inspired ember of forgotten art can be fanned into a flame again!

- Go to an art store and spend an hour or two just looking around. It is amazing how much inspiration you can get just from creative materials! Let your Guardian Angel guide you to tools or materials that feel right. Spend a little money on something and go home and create!

- Go see, hear, and read art! Expose yourself to different types of art that challenge you a bit. Go see things and hear things and read just to widen your range and open your mind to new things! Every concert, opera, or art show will give you the valuable experience of seeing how other Guardian Angels express their creative spirit!

- Set aside an hour or so a week to make art! It may just be doodles or some haiku or photographs or a painting or....? Anything you do in a creative and positive fashion can be art! There are literally thousands of things you can do, from paper-making to writing a play! Create!

Feel uninspired? Here is a simple creative exercise designed to open your mind and spirit and inspire you through the help of your Guardian Angel!

Exercise 12: Creative Inspiration

Sit in a quiet place in a comfortable chair. You may be inside or outside. Have before you the kinds of artistic tools or items you will use to make art. It can be anything at all, really! Even a computer if you plan to write!

You will also need:

- A leaf of a fresh herb, any kind is fine;
- A heavily scented flower, a rose is perfect;
- A small and very beautiful work of art (a small sculpture or painting);
- A favorite stone or shell;
- A bell of some sort, or chimes.

When you are ready, breathe deeply and surround yourself with white light. Banish all stress and negative feelings—let them all go. When you feel relaxed and peaceful, silently call upon your Guardian Angel to come and help you. Touch your artistic tools and say:

Holy Guardian Angel
Muse of art and creation
Inspire my imagination
Fill me with inspiration

Ring the bell and say:

Come as the spirit of sound
That all I hear may be art!

Look at the art piece intensely, say:

Come as the spirit of sight
That all I see may be art!

Chew and taste the herb, say:

Come as the spirit of taste
That all I consume may be art!

Smell the flower deeply, say:

Come as the spirit of scent
That all I smell may be art!

Touch and caress the stone or shell carefully, say;

Come as the spirit of feeling
That all I touch may be art!

Now sit quietly, eyes and all senses closed, and let all the things you have just experienced wash over you and through you and open the doors to all your senses. Pray to your Guardian Angel as you like. When you are ready to create, say:

Holy Guardian Angel
Muse of art and creation
Inspire my imagination
Fill me with inspiration
Fiat lux! **(Let there be light!)**

Now create something! Keep creating! Create every day, week, month, and year! Make art a part of your life and you will always be surrounded by divine inspiration! Remember: Art will bring you closer to your Guardian Angel than almost anything else you can do. It is never a waste of time. Want to instantly communicate with your Guardian Angel? Then go create and be inspired!

Chapter 6:

Balancing Your Relationship
with Your Guardian Angel

If you have been following the preceding chapters and increasing the intensity and frequency of your communication with your Guardian Angel, then it is time to pause in the process and look at how it affects you and your life so that you are not overwhelmed. Balance in this process is very important to your comfort, to the success of your spiritual evolution, and to the success of this divine relationship!

Communication with your Guardian Angel will influence your life through the balance of knowledge, will, and action. If you follow your angel's lead, your personal growth and evolution can proceed at an astonishing and yet balanced and acceptable rate.

Real knowledge is self-knowledge, and your Guardian Angel *is* your Higher Self. True knowledge of things offers concrete guidance and information and reveals important patterns, but you may have to decode the messages contained therein. With practice, this process becomes easier and easier. The flow of information will always go two ways, however. As you grow closer to your Guardian Angel, your knowledge and inspiration will increase. Your angel will indicate books, movies, articles, and paths of study that are important for your personal spiritual growth. Each step always leads to the next one.

Doing what you are really supposed to do, God's will as it were, is the hardest thing on the planet. Yet this is what your Guardian Angel will unceasingly urge you to do. From birth to death, you are pushed and pulled by parents, friends, society, organizations, and traditions to do and believe certain things. Once you have found the inner guidance of your angel, your True Will soon becomes clearer and clearer. Great thinkers, great artists, holy men and women, all fought great prejudice, hardship, and outrage to follow their True Wills. With the help of your Guardian Angel, so will you.

As your bond with your angel becomes stronger, clear inspirations and encouragement will be given. What should you do? Your angel may suggest a pilgrimage, taking up painting, bungee jumping, donating time to help the homeless, taking more time to play with your children, or any number of other new actions of which others may disapprove. Sometimes when you ask for divine guidance, what is offered is very different from what you expect. You have to learn that it is foolish to simply ignore such unexpected advice. Learning to practice what you preach can be a very difficult thing. Only God knows what you need to do and be to grow and fulfill your work on this Earth, and it is the job of your Guardian Angel to instruct and advise you.

PETITIONING YOUR GUARDIAN ANGEL

So far, we have explored ways you can receive help and guidance from your Guardian Angel. Once you have succeeded in this, you may begin to ask your angel for specific help or information! As in any teacher/student relationship, listening to what the teacher has to say is most important. Indeed, listening and heeding the guidance and support your angel is willing and able to provide you may be enough for you. In that case, you can remain silent and maintain this one-way relationship. But if you want to take the relationship between you and your angel to a new level, then your voice must be heard. You must find a way to petition your Guardian Angel to answer your questions and fill whatever needs you have.

The most obvious way to do this, as in the classroom, is to raise your hand and ask. With a Guardian Angel, this takes the form of active prayer, of simply asking your question or stating your need in clear images and feelings. A number of meditations and exercises have been presented in previous chapters. Simply take the one you like best and, within it, create a time where you petition or ask questions of your angel. Then be ready for an answer. The answer may be a dream. It may be a coincidence, or arrive as a call from a friend. You may use an oracle to ask the question. The choice is yours.

The key here is that you establish clarity of mind, body, and spirit before asking anything of your Guardian Angel. Here are some basic rules for doing that:

- Do not bother your Guardian Angel with silly, pointless questions or questions whose answers you already know or can find on your own. For example, don't ask for a winning lottery number or for an update on Aunt Mabel's health. These are insulting and, as it says in the Bible, "The Lord is not mocked lightly." Your angel exists to guide and help you, not humor your silliness or indulge your laziness. Real questions, real needs, and real calls for help will always be answered, as long as they involve your spiritual growth and welfare.

- Frame your questions or petitions in very simple images and symbols. Remember, you are communicating with a being that is spiritually far beyond anything human. Keep it direct and simple. Questions like, What should I do next? How can I help others? and How can I solve my anger problem?, are all clear and easy to communicate with emotion and focus.

- Think long and hard about your questions or petitions before placing them before your Guardian Angel. Meditate on the wording. Ask your self: Do I really need divine help with this or can I deal with it on my own? Refine your request. Examine your motives! Make sure that they are spiritual in nature and partake of love.

Energetic and focused prayer within a meditative or contemplative exercise is very effective. What follows are several specific exercises for petitioning your Guardian Angel:

Exercise 13: Letter Writing

On a nice piece of paper with a nice pen, write your Guardian Angel a letter. It should be short and sweet, detailing what it is you need to know. It should not be trivial or silly, like asking for a lotto number! It should be something you really *will* to know for your spiritual advancement. With love and good manners, write out the whole question and explanation, sign it, and fold it.

If the question has to do with emotions, take the letter and sink it in a body of water. If it has to with material goods, bury it at the foot of a tree. If it has to do with the intellect or learning, take it to a high place and let it fly away (use a small piece of paper so you don't impact the environment). When you do this, say a prayer—something like:

Guardian Angel
Let me see the truth
Give me knowledge I seek
That I may grow
In body, mind, and spirit!

Wait for your answer. Be very aware of your reality. The answer may not come in a way you expect, but if you have made a connection with your Guardian Angel at this point, you will know the answer when you see/hear/read/feel it. Remember: Your Guardian Angel can take the form of anyone and anything in your reality. Be open and you will see the answer. It will then be up to you to accept or reject what your angel is offering you. But remember again: You asked! If you do not like the answer, look to your self and your own ego. If you reject what your angel is telling you, what you know is true, do not expect much more help from your angel until you are in a more receptive state of mind!

A friend used this method to ask why she was having migraine headaches that had no apparent cause. A week later she discovered she had food allergies.

Exercise 14: Sigil Writing

Take a piece of paper and a pen. Write your question in one sentence. Cross off all of the letters that repeat (example: Why do I overeat? = WHYDOIVERAT?) Now, take the remaining letters and create a sigil or symbol with them. The above example might look like this:

Now comes the hard part. Draw this symbol on a small piece of paper, and throw all the other writing away. Light a white candle and call to your Guardian Angel as you have already learned to do. Now pray to your Guardian Angel; pray hard and long, fill your prayer with the *need* to know the answer to your question. When you have reached an emotional frenzy, concentrating all the time on your sigil, burn the sigil in the candle flame. As you do so, see yourself giving this glowing symbol to your Guardian Angel. Your angel takes it and fades away. Breathe, meditate until you are calm, pray, and thank your Guardian Angel. Then blow out the candle. Your answer will come.

My answer came over the next week in three different magazines in which I "happened" to read the same message: "Most people overeat under stress." My Guardian Angel had placed the answer directly in front of me, so I couldn't possibly miss it: Lower the stress in your life and you will not overeat. I have been doing this and it works!

Let me explain how this process further plays out in one's life with an example. I gained weight over a decade and it began to impact my life in ways I did not like. My Guardian Angel kept shoving people and resources at me to give me clear knowledge of what that impact was. I knew, clearly, that my will was to get into shape, but, like many, I saw a number of reasons why I couldn't. My job took too much time; I didn't have the money to join a club; I only wanted to do certain types of exercise; I had book deadlines. Sound familiar?

So I asked my Guardian Angel with a sigil: I *know* what I need to do, but I don't know how to *do* it? Can you help me? Voila! I got a new boss that week who turned out to be a gym fanatic and talked incessantly about the benefits of working out. My work schedule suddenly became flexible, so I had the time to exercise. Still, I put it off and put it off. Finally, a former coworker visited my office for business and we chatted. At the end, he gave me a free one-month membership to a gym two blocks away! How could I not act?! It's been nine months and I'm still a member of that gym and I feel better than I have in years.

Exercise 15: Requesting a Plan of Action

If you are clear on what you need to do, if you know you Will to do something, but feel stuck or blocked and need some help from your Guardian Angel to *act* on a situation, problem, or goal, try this.

Take a piece of paper and, with a red pen, write the following:

I know...

I will...

So I must act by...

Under each one of these headings except the last one, write about your problem. For instance:

I know
I can write well
I will
to be a published journalist
So I must act by
?

Breathe deeply, close your eyes, and surround yourself with white light. Call upon your Guardian Angel in any way you wish. See your Guardian Angel come and sit by you, one arm about your shoulder. It is here to help you. As you surround yourself with the power and light of your angel say something like:

Guardian Angel
Banish all guilt
Banish all doubts
Banish all excuses

Banish all obstacles
Show me the truth
Show me the way
To act with love and will
That I may succeed every day!

Meditate silently on what you have written on your paper, then as ideas pop into your head from your Guardian Angel, begin to list possible actions under the last heading. Write at least six, but you may become inspired and write many more! Listen in silence; your angel is answering your request!

When you are done, take the list of actions and write numbers next to the ones you are really able to do. Start with the easiest and end with the hardest. Meditate on this list with your Guardian Angel for a while. It may want you to make some changes, add or subtract a few things. Now, you have a plan of action!

On the following page is an example of a plan of action that I built in this way with the help of my Guardian Angel.

I know	**I will**	**so I must act by**
I can write well	to be a published journalist	3. Write in a journal daily to practice
		14. Start writing for local/school papers
		2. Get a good computer
		11. Have friends look at my writing
		12. Join a writing group
		4. Take a journalism class
		5. Buy books on how to submit articles
		6. Research the market
		10. Make time every day to write
		9. Create a list of subjects I wish to write about
		7. Find out what sells
		13. Set writing deadlines for myself
		8. Talk to other successful writers
		1. Clear my desk
		15. Set up stuff to submit articles (envelopes, etc.)
		16. Write/submit x# of articles a month

My final plan of action:

1. Clear my desk
2. Get a good computer
3. Write in a journal daily to practice
4. Take a journalism class
5. Buy books on how to submit articles
6. Research the market
7. Find out what sells
8. Talk to other successful writers
9. Create a list of subjects I wish to write about
10. Make time every day to write
11. Have friends look at my writing
12. Join a writing group
13. Set writing deadlines for myself
14. Start writing for local/school papers
15. Set up stuff to submit articles (envelopes, etc.)
16. Write/submit a certain number of articles a month

Once you have created your final action plan, close your eyes, ask for help, support, and guidance from your angel in doing these things. For every step you take, your angel will be there to help clear the way. Breathe deeply and feel the light center in your heart. See it as an arrow of light. Clap once and see it fly. You have already begun!

Begin *that day* to do the first thing on the list. You are now on a path of divinely inspired action. If something doesn't work out, move around or over the problem. Nothing is easy! Your Guardian Angel will *not* do the work for you! You are on this Earth to learn and grow, and you can only do that by striving, working, playing, making mistakes, and learning from them. Go forward! Your Guardian Angel will help you in ways you cannot even imagine. Accept advice, clues, opportunities, and help from whatever direction they come. Often they will come from unexpected sources or people! Keep your mind open; your Guardian Angel is everywhere!

Part 3:

Merging with Your Guardian Angel

Chapter 7:

Your Guardian Angel and Your Shadow

One thing that every faith and tradition teaches is that there is a balance to the cosmos: light and dark, good and evil, yin and yang, male and female, positive and negative. Everything, it is said, is composed of opposites and everything has a dual nature. In fact, it seems that uniting opposites is the general rule of the universe. This is the biological model of continuation of the species (man and woman unite in a child) and, more important, the internal model of consciousness (conscious mind and subconscious mind unite in the Self).

Where does your Guardian Angel fall in this duality? Is it of heaven or Earth? We know it is of good and of God, but what of its relationship to evil, to darkness? If you have a supreme Higher Self, do you also have a lower self, a demon that abides with you? In fact, your Guardian Angel does have a shadow, as do all things.

My many years of exploring this question have led me to three conclusions:

Your dark side, or Shadow, must be discussed when talking about your Guardian Angel or Higher Self.

Your Shadow and the ignorance it manifests are very real and concrete parts of the world, but they begin and end within you. They are not a part of nature.

Merging with your Guardian Angel includes balancing it with your Shadow. Neglecting this can make you unbalanced and egomaniacal!

THE REALITY OF EVIL

What is evil? It is causing pain to other living beings without a compelling need to do so. It is a real and tangible essence, just as love, anger, and peace are real tangible essences. Nature does not manifest evil; evil comes from us. Animals generally do not do evil. Their killing and aggression are all rooted in basic needs and instincts. Animals, for the most part (except for some primates), do not engage in sadistic or evil actions.

Most religions agree that evil comes with self-consciousness, the awareness that you have a choice to do good or evil. Many traditions say this consciousness derives from a primeval "fall from grace." Some say it manifested when the human species reached a certain point of evolution, when the right and left brains began to interact. Or possibly it was the result of a neurological evolution that developed centers of ego and self-awareness.

If evil is part of the human condition and began with a fall from grace in the distant past, it must be by God's design. That must mean that we each carry this challenge of good and evil within us, since we ourselves bring it into the world. If this is so, and if your Guardian Angel is relevant and experiential, then there must be a dark reflection of your Guardian Angel within and below you, just as there is one within and above you. And in fact, there is. Jung called it the Shadow. Others have called it the devil or the demon. Just as you have a seed or ray of the light of God within you and bonded to you—your Guardian Angel—you also have a dark side, a seed of darkness, a source of negative thoughts and deeds. All those cartoons showing a little angel on one shoulder and a devil on the other were true all along!

God made you in his/her own image. You contain the universe and the contradictions and impossibilities and mysteries of the cosmos as well. *As without, so within.* Therefore you carry the problem of the light and shadow, good and evil, into the world with you—by the grace of God, I might add!

How does this affect the entire process of finding and uniting with your Guardian Angel? Simply that your awareness of your Self, of all you are and have experienced, must also extend into your Shadow, or your dark side. While the job of your Guardian Angel is to help you attain awareness and consciousness, this cannot be done without clearly coming to grips with your Shadow—all the things about you that are not positive, helpful, or based on love.

What is the source of your Shadow? Simply put, it is your ego and your misplaced animal self. The job of your ego is to create a persona or self-image that you can use to operate in the world. It is your point of reference in the physical universe. Your ego's job is to keep you alive and safe and provide you with all the good things in life—food, shelter, pleasure, attention, and love. Your ego does a great job if you live well and are happy and live in balance with others, society, and the world. Yet, in the end, it has a job to do: to look out for "Number One"—that is, *you.* It does not care about other people.

If your ego is balanced, then you live a self-interested life, but are also aware of what is right and wrong. When your pleasures and desires conflict with others, you resolve those conflicts fairly. When your ego is out of control, when the influence of your Self is weak, then evil can manifest as your desires and demands overtake compassion and common sense.

Your Guardian Angel can help you here. When you have a direct connection with the divine through your Guardian Angel, your ego is kept in check. This is, of course, the ideal. Your ego and your Guardian Angel have their battles. We always want more than is good for us: more food, more money, more power, more attention and adulation! It is your Guardian Angel that provides your conscience, the moral compass that keeps your ego from pushing beyond its natural domain.

This deep internal and external tension between your ego and your angel can be found in any many myths that depict the Solar Hero versus the dark entity of Evil. Horus fought and conquered Set; Marduk fought and conquered Tiamat; Woten fought and conquered the Midguard Serpent; Theseus killed the Minotaur; and St. George killed the Dragon. All these heroes and gods of light reflect the Guardian Angel, golden, winged, representing the power of heaven and of the Creator. All the dark gods, often dragons or horned animal gods, represent the ego, the dark side, the unfettered animal mind within you that also seeks to guide you!

For all the fear it inspires, your Shadow is as much a part of you as your Guardian Angel. Without it you would not have the aggressiveness to succeed at difficult tasks; you would not have the power and joy of the sex drive to make life so pleasurable and so very interesting! Without your dark side, you would not have the self-love that helps you through dark times; you would not have the "edge" that comes out in such creative ways to express the human condition.

You may deny this, yet in your heart of hearts, you know that there are light and shadow within you. This is not bad; it is natural. Your ego, rightfully balanced, is important. People with weak egos are unable to function at all. Your ego serves a purpose. If it didn't, God would not have made it manifest!

Evil, on the other hand, is the ego run amok; it is the Shadow overruling the Guardian Angel. It is the human choice of flesh and self-interest over spirit and love. It needs to be fought and held at bay. But evil is a flexible idea meaning different things to different people in different circumstances. Remember: Evil is not the Shadow, it is the *preponderance* of the Shadow, or the Shadow out of balance. This manifests differently in different people. Just as your Guardian Angel is unique and different, so too is your Shadow and the problems or challenges it offers.

For example, if you have a strong sex drive, this can be a positive thing if channeled by your Guardian Angel in an appropriate way. God created sex for both procreation and enjoyment. Yet inappropriate sexuality, driven by an inflated ego that somehow justifies self-gratification over all else, leads to evils like molestation. In fact, it seems that those who have attained the greatest success and power often fall prey in the worst ways to their egos. And there is an important message here.

As your Guardian Angel grows, so does your awareness of your Shadow and its potential to use or abuse your ego. Your Guardian Angel, the source of all awareness, is *not* the ultimate enemy of your Shadow; it is the regulator of your Shadow that balances and, in the end, supercedes it. Though St. George killed the dragon, the dragon survives. The battle between light and darkness is more like a dance, a flow between yin and yang.

Since *everything* was created by God and since your Guardian Angel is the seed emanation of God in you, it follows that your Shadow is, in the end, linked to your Guardian Angel. It is the part that is unconscious, the part that offers obstacles, problems, pain, and suffering to you so that you may learn and grow. Your Shadow is not *of* the Guardian Angel, but it is part of the path of the Guardian Angel. It is, in fact, the Shadow of your Guardian Angel that is cast within your deep mind and where the demon ego mutters "Me, me, me!!!" Balanced, it is an important teacher. Given all power, it leads to horrific evil.

Why is knowing this vital to your goal of uniting with your Guardian Angel? Because this dance of light and shadow happens every day in the world around you, as well as within you. You struggle with moral and ethical decisions daily. Do you give in to your animal nature or resist? Do you think of yourself before others? Are you needlessly cruel or do you extend kindness to another? These are not philosophical or abstract questions. They are real decisions that affect everyone and everything around you. In general, it is easier to give in to the Shadow then to heed the sometimes-difficult advice of your Guardian Angel. Your Higher Self tells you to "love your neighbor as yourself," but your ego, your territorial animal nature or Shadow, says "look out for Number One and forget your neighbor."

When you seek union with your Guardian Angel and ignore your dark side, your selfish and self-centered animal self, you create a split in your world. We have all met people like this—"white lighters," or very positive people who seem to glow with spirituality and religious fervor. Yet they turn around and gossip, slander, or commit adultery and never see the contradiction in themselves! We look at such people and label them hypocrites, yet the truth is far more complex. They have worked hard at connecting with their Guardian Angels, yet they have ignored and tried to exorcise their Shadow. Unfortunately, this is impossible to do, because their Shadows are part of them.

Brave and balanced spiritual seekers confront and accept the reality of their Shadows without giving in to them or letting them rule their actions. If you behave in a certain way or have certain dark feelings, thoughts, or desires, do not suppress them; confront and deal with them. They exist for a reason. They are all lessons to learn. You may hate parts of yourself, but that alone will not help. Invoke your Guardian Angel to help you understand and balance your Shadow.

As you face your Shadow—and you will have to do so as you become closer and closer to your Guardian Angel—ask yourself two questions:

- Is this a behavior, neurosis, or desire that I need to eliminate or substantially change? If so, then you need to ask your Guardian Angel how to accomplish this.

- Is this a behavior, neurosis, or desire that is of the Shadow, but that I can live with? If the answer is yes, then ask your Guardian Angel how it can be embraced, accepted, and turned into something positive and life-affirming.

The rule of thumb is this: If your ego/Shadow causes pain to other living beings through selfishness or self-centeredness or ignorance except in dire necessity (i.e., self-defense), then it is a behavior or tendency or habit that needs to be severely changed or eliminated.

Keep in mind that you are dealing with psychic dynamite here. Only you know your inner demon, your Shadow. Professionals can help you explore the tunnels of your inner mind, but only you can slay or transform the dragons that lurk there. The ultimate weapon in this struggle is love under Will—the power of your Guardian Angel.

There are traditionally five key components to your Shadow or dark side. Confronting and "piercing" these dark aspects is the spiritual work you do on the path of spiritual growth. These negative parts of your personality, which some call sins, are called *kleshas* in Sanskrit. They are ignorance, egotism, attachment, repulsion, and clinging to life. Your Shadow manifests chiefly in the varied forms of the kleshas. Meditating on them and how you can move beyond them can help you keep your Shadow in check. The most important thing is that you are aware of how the Shadow manifests in your life and how your Guardian Angel can help you overcome and learn from aspects of yourself that are part of your dark side.

IGNORANCE

Ignorance is more than not knowing something; it is also refusing to admit what you don't know. Most evil in the world is done out of ignorance. People cause tremendous evil by being ignorant about other people, other cultures, other religions, and how others feel or think. People also commit great evil when they are ignorant of consequences, of natural laws, and of the long-term reactions that follow from their actions.

Thinking that there is one law or one way for all people is the height of ignorance and has led to most of the religious wars down through history, and even today. Ignorance of self is to blame for most of the misguided actions people commit to make themselves feel more powerful, more secure, happier, or more important. All of these misguided feelings and actions are promoted by the ego, which seeks to put your perceived needs over the needs of all others. Being open to learning new things and challenging assumptions is key to controlling this instinct, the key to spiritual growth.

EGOTISM

Selfishness, self-centeredness, an inflated view of how wonderful or beautiful or smart you are—all of these contribute to the poison called egotism. The moment you think that you are better than other human beings or somehow above them, you have separated yourself from your own humanity and opened the door for your Shadow to take control. Racism, bigotry, intolerance, and a host of other true evils are generated from egotism. Others use this character flaw to unite groups of ignorant people into lynch mobs and other larger aggressive mass movements. Through flattery and threats, others can use your egotism to control and manipulate you. Almost all advertising is based on this simple idea! Pride indeed goes before a fall, and constantly seeing yourself as wonderful and beyond reproach effectively blinds you from seeing yourself objectively and correcting flaws in your character. Egotism is the root of much delusion!

ATTACHMENT

Attachment, in this context, means to covet or desire something beyond what is natural. Everything you desire, wish for, or want is an attachment that takes part of your spirit. If you are not careful, when you attach yourself to a thing or person, you give that thing or person power over you. In this way you can be manipulated, carried this way and that like a leaf in a stream. When you develop attachments, you give up your Will; you begin to define your happiness and satisfaction by the getting or acquiring of the things you desire. Then, once you have them, the attachment grows. They become so important that you begin to live your life and make basic decisions based on the things or people to which you are attached, not on love or your True Will.

Attachment can trap you in miserable jobs, terrible relationships, and absurd living situations. The very things that make you deeply unhappy are often the things you thought you desired. Thank your ego for that! The point is this: Spirit is not a *thing*; nor is love, joy, or all the truly important things in life. You are told daily that buying things will make you happy, but does it? Maybe for a short time, but then the craving begins again. Nothing is ever quite enough and then you make evil choices and decisions in order to get more, to keep what you have, and to fight off all rivals. In the end, all things pass away. What is left? This is what your Guardian Angel is trying to tell you. Yes, enjoy the things in your life, but never mistake them for what is real: spirit, love, will, and joy.

REPULSION

Just as attraction is the root of so much evil and misguided acquisitiveness, so repulsion is the root of much evil born from fear. In this context, repulsion means anything that you dislike or that repels you. This could be anything from heights and spiders, to people from different cultures and of different religions.

Books have been written on why we have irrational fears, such as a fear of darkness or snakes. It is, in the end, not important why we have these fears. The point is that each fear provides an opportunity to grow and evolve. If a phobia does not bother you, then it is not urgent that you work on it. But if it is a problem, then it must be faced. Why? Because somehow it is a key to unlocking a part of your Shadow that is hindering you. It is a lesson to learn, something on your path you are offered to work out and move beyond. Your Guardian Angel exists to help you do this.

I managed to overcome my extreme fear of heights somewhat (I'll never be over it completely) by rappelling down cliffs with a roommate who "happened" to love mountain climbing. This was the help my Guardian Angel offered and I took it. Terrifying? Yes. But the joy and self-worth I gained from challenging this part of my Shadow was amazing! It allowed me to move on in other ways I hadn't even thought of!

Repulsion is not always inborn or focused on things, however. In general, people fear the unknown and assume that the way they were raised is the best way to live on this planet. Ethnocentrism, bigotry, and persecutions are all outgrowths of repulsion.

Is there a more insidious evil? Hate literature often depicts targeted groups as repulsive. Jews and African Americans were said to eat human flesh, kill children, and undermine society. Absurd! Targeted groups are always shown as disfigured, dirty, with evil faces, because racists and other bigots know that repulsion is a major component of the Shadow. Make a person or group of people seem repulsive and people will fear them. Fear leads to anger, anger to violence. This evil must be challenged.

Your Guardian Angel will help you look below the surface to see the essential similarities between all human beings and to accept differences. Getting past repulsion is key, because if you let your dislikes control your emotions, they become governed by outside forces, and you can be manipulated and controlled. Then you lose your Will. Your Guardian Angel can help you meet repulsion with compassion, hold your repulsion back until you can be educated, and remain open to changing your opinions about things. Remember, tarantulas, no matter how repulsive, are actually gentle and affectionate pets!

CLINGING TO LIFE

People will do amazing and horrific things to avoid the threat of death. Leaders have gone to war over this fear, people sacrifice others, push people out of lifeboats, and, in short, often do whatever it takes to survive. This survival instinct is natural; it is a key purpose of your ego to ensure your survival. But when fear of death becomes obsessive or when you are willing to harm others unnecessarily to avoid threats, something is wrong.

Death is a part of nature. It is not only inescapable, it is also one of the great lessons you must face at the end of your life. It is natural to wish to avoid death and to live the best you can. It is not normal to have an obsessive preoccupation with prolonging life no matter what the cost to others. Because your Guardian Angel was born with you and will accompany you past the veil of death, it exists to help you to accept death and to come to terms with it in a positive and life-affirming way.

Following are two simple exercises for confronting and dealing with your Shadow and aspects of it. As you become closer with your Guardian Angel, you will need to become more and more conscious of your Shadow. Your Guardian Angel stands ready and able to help you in this challenging but crucial process.

Exercise 16: Piercing the Kleshas

The goal of this exercise is to focus your attention and the attention of your Guardian Angel on your kleshas so that you will be better able to "pierce" them and be aware of them as they emerge in your life. You will need a quiet place, a white candle in a candleholder, five small (palm-sized) pieces of gray paper, a little salt, a small dark ceramic bowl, and a black marker pen. You may also want to burn a little sage or other incense.

First, take a quiet bath in which you have sprinkled some salt. Afterwards, sit quietly facing north, with the papers and candle before you. Sprinkle salt all about you and say:

Out, out. Throughout and about
All good come in; all evil stay out.

Sit in the dark and think about the kleshas, those negative unbalanced aspects of your dark side or Shadow. Think of how they have emerged and hindered and harmed you in the past. Light the candle and pray or chant to your Guardian Angel. Say something like:

Guardian Angel
Come to me
Fill me with light
Unveil my sight
Reveal my Shadow
That I may see.

Take up the pen and write each of these words at the top of a separate piece of paper: *Ignorance, Attraction, Repulsion, Anger,* and *Clinging to life*. On the back of each of these papers, write how that klesha has hindered or harmed you in the past. For ignorance, for example, you may write *Gossiping* or *Intolerance*. What you write is up to you and will be unique. When done, place the pages about the candle and think deeply about all five of them. Ask your Guardian Angel to help you overcome and move beyond them day to day. Then, one by one, burn the papers and let the ashes fall into the bowl. As you do so, say:

Holy Guardian Angel,
Be here now
Banish all evil
Remove all fear
Replace ignorance with knowledge
Calm the fires of attraction
Make me more accepting of that which repels me
Replace my anger with peace
And lead me to accept the end of life
By the power of the love and will you embody!

When you are done, see the room fill with the white light of your Guardian Angel. Pray for specific changes in your behavior and thinking that you feel you need to make. Let the weight of the kleshas fall from your shoulders with the help of your Guardian Angel. When done, scatter a little salt about you and once again say:

Out, out. Through and about

All good come in, all evil stay out.

Then go and bury the ashes at the foot of a tree.

In the next meditation you will face your Shadow or dark side and give your Guardian Angel, the emanation of God, dominion over it. This is a very simplified and modern version of an ancient ritual calling upon the force of God to subdue the force of evil.

Exercise 17: Confronting Your Shadow

Do this exercise in a dark room where you will not be disturbed. You may sit on the floor or on a chair. You will need a mirror big enough to see your face. You will also need a little salt and two candles, one white and one black. Put each in a candleholder and set them on either side of the mirror. Take a quiet bath in which you have sprinkled some salt.

When ready, go to the room. Sit quietly facing north, facing the mirror. Sprinkle salt all about you and say:

Out, out. Throughout and about
All good come in, all evil stay out.

Now, pray or chant to your Guardian Angel, asking it to come and aid you in this work. Say something like:

Guardian Angel
Come to me
Fill me with light
Unveil my sight
Reveal the Shadow
That I may see!

Light both candles, saying something like:

Light calls to darkness
Darkness shadows light
I balance between them
Evil and right.
May light overcome
And rule the Shadow
Let it be done!

Gaze into the mirror at your reflection. Bring to mind all the evil and self-centered things you have done. Call forth your small, selfish, ego-centered self! Soon your facial image will darken. Think all the common bad thoughts you

ponder, examine your darkest fantasies and the terrible things you feel and think
but never talk about. In short, let your Shadow appear in your reflection. When
you see the face of your Shadow in your reflection—and it may be shocking—
quickly take up the marker and draw an upward-pointing triangle about it,
saying:

By my angel
By the light
By all that's good
By all that's right
I conjure, trap,
And subjugate thee
To be ruled by my angel
So may it be!

Call upon your Guardian Angel and see the triangle you have drawn surrounded
by pure light! Pray or chant to your Guardian Angel to rule over, control, and
subjugate your Shadow so that you may grow and find real happiness and success. As you do this, draw a circle around the triangle, then place a dot in the
center of the triangle/circle.

Breathe deeply and feel the darkness covered by the light. The Shadow never
disappears, but is now utterly controlled by the light. Let the light fill you, ban-
ishing all bits of Shadow, evil thoughts, and feelings, until you are calm and
peaceful and filled with light. Say something like:

Guardian Angel
Praise to thee
Control my Shadow
And set me free
Forever guide and protect
Always help me
As we will
So may it be!

Blow out the candles and wipe the marker off the mirror with a damp paper towel.
Scatter a little salt all about you and on the mirror and once again say:

Out, out. Throughout and about
All good come in, all evil stay out.

Then go and bury the paper towel at the foot of a tree.

THE PRINCE OF LIES

The dark side or Shadow is sometimes personified as the Prince of Lies. This is a good characterization, but for different reasons than have been noted in most religious texts. We lie best when we lie to ourselves. Many cartoons are filled with such observations and we find them funny, except when they apply to us! Here are several lies I told myself today; see if they seem familiar.

"I think I lost some weight."

"I wasn't really speeding."

"I can't afford to contribute to that charity now."

"I didn't know that would be a problem for you."

"It isn't really gossiping..."

The Shadow lives amid lies and justifications. You expressed your anger inappropriately? You lied to yourself and said things like, "That person deserved it"? You cheated on taxes? You lied and said you deserved it? You missed an appointment or made an error at work? You convinced yourself that it was not your fault!

Self-deception is the greatest deception. One of the greatest services your Guardian Angel does for you is to shine the light of truth on everything you do and say. God provided you with a Guardian Angel as a cosmic reality check. This is not always a comfortable situation, but then growth and learning are not always pleasant, and the universe is a tough teacher.

How does this unfold in your day-to-day dealings with your Guardian Angel? Through an aspect of the angel that you know well: your conscience. The problem is that you do not always listen to it. Yet every time you lie, cheat, steal, gossip, or in other ways manifest your Shadow, your Guardian Angel is there to let you know the truth. As you create a stronger and stronger bond with your angel, your awareness of this inner voice will grow. As you communicate more and more with your angel, the truth will become more and more obvious to you when you transgress and do things you know are wrong. Again, this is between you and your Guardian Angel!

No one has the right to tell you what is right or wrong, what you should or should not do. Yes, murder is wrong, but not if you are a soldier defending your home. You are completely unique, as is your Will; none will ever tread the path you tread or learn the lessons you need to learn from the universe. Your morals are embodied in the word of God that is your Guardian Angel. Your angel is the embodiment of truth and righteousness. Because no one knows your heart like God, no one else can pass judgment.

YOUR TRUE GUARDIAN ANGEL

Because your Shadow or ego is the Prince of Lies, it will do its best to help you deceive yourself. If you make a concerted effort to connect and bond with your Guardian Angel, your Shadow will immediately try to deceive you into believing that *it* is your angel. Therefore it is of the utmost importance that you use prayer, meditation, and visualization to learn to recognize the real feel and tone of your Guardian Angel. Keep the following in mind:

- Your Guardian Angel will never order you to do anything. The divine plan for humans revolves around Free or True Will. Your angel will only nudge, suggest, offer, and warn. If you feel a spiritual entity ordering you to do this or that, it is not your Guardian Angel.

- Your Guardian Angel always manifests or communicates through a feeling of love.

- Your Guardian Angel will never recommend that you commit mental, physical, or spiritual violence against a living being or harm another— no matter what.

- Your Guardian Angel exists to guide, help, and teach, never punish. To repeat, your angel will never punish you for doing or not doing something. This does not mean that action or inaction cannot cause pain; they can. But your angel is not responsible for such action or inaction; you are. Your angel will merely try to warn or help you.

- Your Guardian Angel will never suggest you do something you know is wrong, like steal. This does not mean that your angel will not help you open your mind to accept things you previously rejected. Guidance from your angel may even lead you to make changes in your life you once rejected. The point is, your angel will never push you to do some thing you know is immoral or against your core beliefs.

- Your Guardian Angel will *never* curse or harm another at your bidding: It is impossible! Your angel is divine, an emanation of God. As such, it is pure love.

- Your Guardian Angel will never build up your ego. Let me clarify: Your Guardian Angel will never tell you that you are better, smarter, more beautiful, or more holy than other people. This does not mean that your angel will not help you see what a great person you are. It just means your angel will never tell you that you are superior to others. Never. In God's eyes, all people are blessed.

- Your Guardian Angel will let you learn at your own pace, even if it means stumbling over a particular life-lesson over and over. Your angel will not push or impel you to learn something faster than you are able to handle.

If a being asserts it is your Guardian Angel and then does any of these negative things, it is *not* your angel talking; it is your ego or animal self, the great deceiver, wearing a mask in order to trick you.

How can you be sure that you are communing with your Guardian Angel and not with your ego or Shadow or some other subversive part of your inner mind? Here are three simple techniques for making sure that you are working with your Guardian Angel and not another entity. Remember: If you have worked carefully through prayer and meditation to connect with your Guardian Angel, then you know the feel of your angel, just like you know the voice of an old friend when he or she calls you. If you take time to really understand and recognize the essence of your Guardian Angel as you build up a bond, you will never be deceived.

Exercise 18: Identifying Your Guardian Angel through Light

Before you make contact with your Guardian Angel, do deep breathing and fill your space and your body with white light. Make sure that your mind, heart, and body are clear of any serious imbalance or negative emotion and that you are reasonably comfortable and at peace. Make the white light a shield or "egg" of power around you. Pray to the divine to purify you. When your Guardian Angel appears, cover it with this white light and divine energy. If it is really your Guardian Angel, it will draw strength and joy from this stream of divine energy. If it fades away, it was not really your angel. Follow the same directions when you feel or hear the presence of your angel, but fill yourself and your surrounding area with divine white light. Again, if the presence leaves you, it was not your Guardian Angel.

Exercise 19: Identifying Your Guardian Angel through Prayer

Before communing with your Guardian Angel, sprinkle salt about you or bathe in water with salt in it. Salt removes negative energies of all kinds and banishes evil. Make sure that you are clean in mind and body before calling upon your angel. You may also wish to perform other simple purifications like burning sage or leaning against a tree and "clearing" yourself before you connect with your angel. Doing these things with prayerful intent or using mantras to call down divine energy will help you eliminate all negativity and open yourself to only the highest vibrations. All forms of meditation, prayer, and yoga will help prepare you for contact with your angel and will keep away all other entities.

Exercise 20: Identifying Your Guardian Angel through Symbols

If you have cause to believe that a force identifying itself as your Guardian Angel is not what it says it is, challenge it. Focus on a religious or magical symbol that has great meaning to you. It may be a cross, the Arabic script for Allah, a Star of David, an upright pentagram, an OM symbol—whatever symbol has the strongest influence on your spiritual path. Visualize this symbol very clearly glowing with white light, hovering at your heart. With as much pure love as you can summon, project that symbol at your Guardian Angel, or simply project it about you if the presence of your angel is not clearly focused. If the being that is communicating with you is really your angel, you will feel a returned blessing of love. If it is not, it will flee.

It is important to note that not everyone who hears voices is hearing the voice of his or her Guardian Angel. All things are indeed spiritual and part of your path, but some phenomena that manifest within your mind are indicative of specific problems that need to be addressed by a professional. I have clearly stated above what your Guardian Angel will and will not do. If you are plagued by the Shadow and these simple techniques do not banish the manifestations, seek professional help. Your Guardian Angel will guide you in this direction as well if it is needed.

THE CHOICE IS YOURS

What about people who choose evil, who seek to embrace and become the Shadow? They most certainly exist; the news is full of them. If they gain the power they seek, they can spread pain and misery to many. These are people who intentionally place the Shadow or ego within the central core of their spiritual being in place of their Guardian Angels. When you choose to place your ego on the throne of your Guardian Angel, you deny your own divinity and embrace the evil of self-centeredness completely, declaring self-gratification and selfishness on all levels as the be-all and end-all of your existence. Then sadly, you wall yourself up in a tower of ego, often consuming more and more, inflicting more and more pain on others, and eventually self-destructing. Why? Because you bind and gag the linchpin of your spiritual life; you shut yourself off from the lifeline of divinity—your Guardian Angel. You consign yourself to the lower spheres of animal pleasures and instincts, seal yourself off forever from real spiritual contact with others and from the embrace of the one being who offers true unconditional love. Isn't this hell?

So much depends on how open you are, how prepared you are to connect with a higher consciousness, and how strong and entrenched your Shadow is. God gave everyone a Guardian Angel—but as a choice, not an imposition. If you are perfectly happy with the simple pleasures of life, that is fine. Your Guardian Angel is here to help and guide you, not push or railroad you. If you wish to grow as a person and to do what you are here to do and learn what you need to learn in this life, then your Guardian Angel will help you. If you do not wish to learn a lesson you are presented with or meet a challenge that is before you, no one will force you to. But that challenge, obstacle, or lesson will not go away.

We are all given the challenges or lessons we need to master. We have as long as we like to accomplish this—a whole lifetime, or beyond, if that is your choice. Yet one thing is clear—your obstacles and challenges will not fade away or disappear. They will be presented to you over and over, often in different formats or ways, until you deal with them, master them, learn from them, and move on. You may remain stuck simply because you either do not see the lesson before you or choose not to deal with it. Then your Guardian Angel can only point out the obvious. Nor can your angel directly help until called upon. At this point, you have two choices: Either you can face the issue, work through it, learn the lesson, and move on; or you can remain in denial, embrace your Shadow, and give up personal responsibility, blaming others or fate.

What can your Guardian Angel do if you refuse to see what is before you? The bottom line? Not much. No one can help you, not even your Guardian Angel, if you do not want to be helped or confront the parts of you that are less than perfect. You choose between the angel and the devil sitting on your shoulders every day. The most sacred thing you have is your Free or True Will—and that includes the will to ignore your Guardian Angel if you wish, or to create conditions that push it away so that it seems absent.

Chapter 8:

Knowledge and Conversation
of the Holy Guardian Angel

You are about to make a great leap. So far, we have explored ways to meet your Guardian Angel and gradually grow closer to it, as well as ways to deal with your Shadow. Until now, this process has been fairly simple. You chose the exercises you wanted to try at your own pace. No pressure. You made the choices.

This is different.

The Knowledge and Conversation of the Holy Guardian Angel requires a full-blown, all-out commitment to experience your Guardian Angel directly on *its* level. It is the culmination of the entire process and of this book. It is also not for everyone. If you are happy with your relationship and communication with your Guardian Angel, then continue on your course and ignore this chapter. If, however, you wish to part the veil and fully experience the intensity and glory of your Guardian Angel, read on.

I will provide two methods for performing the rite of Knowledge and Conversation of the Holy Guardian Angel. In the first, I will lay out the traditional method in fairly modern terms. In the second, I will present a more modern (and faster) method. Both will work *if* you prepare properly and bring to the operation focus, devotion, dedication, will, and a burning desire to connect with your angel. Faith can move mountains and, more important, can open a door between worlds that will allow you direct contact with your Guardian Angel.

Whatever the reality of the Guardian Angel—and different cultures clearly see it differently—this operation works. If it were not effective, it would not have survived as a secret teaching for almost 2000 years through Pagan, Jewish, and Christian mystical traditions, nor would it have appeared in other completely separate cultures such as the Hindu-Tantric tradition of India. I know from personal experience that this rite is real and powerful because I did it successfully and I know of others who have done it as well (see Appendix F). It works. I received Knowledge and Conversation with my angel in 1980 and it has remained my constant daily companion ever since.

OVERVIEW AND HISTORICAL BACKGROUND OF THE RITE

This chapter is, in many ways, the key to and culmination of the entire book. It contains the history and operation of the rite known traditionally as the "Knowledge and Conversation of the Holy Guardian Angel," as well as an ancient and, until now, generally secret ritual known as "The Bornless One."

Simply stated, the goal of this operation is to make your Guardian Angel appear before you in a vision and to communicate with you directly. Essentially, its goal is to break through the barriers that separate you from your Guardian Angel so that you can have direct contact with it. Once accomplished, it is said that you will abide forever with your angel in a close relationship that will benefit you in countless ways.

The Knowledge and Conversation of the Holy Guardian Angel rite is a procedure for systematically calling upon your Guardian Angel in such a way that it causes a breakthrough, the result of which is a mystical and visionary experience of your angel that will change your life forever. You will no longer question the reality of the divine since you will have had firsthand experience of it!

The roots of this spiritual operation lie in ancient traditions that met and merged in Greece and Egypt around the time of Christ. The operation was adopted by Pagans, Christians, and Jews and has, for centuries, been transmitted and adapted by various mystical brotherhoods and sects throughout the West (see Appendix E). As an interesting note, a very similar operation has existed even longer in India. This has recently been published in the West.

To perform the traditional rite, you set up a temple that will be used for the operation, then prepare yourself for a period of time by withdrawing from the world and contemplating the divine in whatever tradition you are most comfortable. The ancient texts say that any religious tradition, including Pagan, Jewish, and Christian, is acceptable, as long as the person is devout and pure. You then begin the actual operation, which, depending on the source cited, lasts from three months to six months. During that time, you lead a meditative life and wholeheartedly concentrate on and invoke your Guardian Angel. You must prepare certain tools and items to use in the rite, and the temple is *never* used during this time for any other purpose. The operation, once begun, must not be abandoned.

During the operation, a special ritual is used from one to four times a day. Traditionally the Bornless One rite has been used by many people in several different forms, but other invocations have been used as well. The key to the rite is a personally written call to your angel. At the end of the established time, the Knowledge and Conversation concludes with an epiphany or peak experience in which your angel will appear as a vision, a voice, or some other overwhelming mystical experience, and will communicate important information to you, bonding with you forever. This lasts three days by most accounts, but some then add a ten-day contemplation period to meditate on and assimilate the experience.

The Knowledge and Conversation of the Guardian Angel has its roots in ancient times. Babylonian, Greek, and Egyptian texts refer to the Guardian Spirit and to rituals used to invoke and communicate with it. The tradition entered or was manifested in Judaism as part of a mystical teaching and finally entered Christian mysticism. The ritual was in circulation in Gnostic times (circa 100 B.C.- 400 A.D.), when all of these magical-religious traditions met and merged in Egypt and Greece, especially in Alexandria. In this magical melting pot we find the origins of both the Knowledge and Conversation of the Guardian Angel operation and of the ritual later called the Bornless One.

The Knowledge and Conversation of the Guardian Angel evolved through four distinct phases that can be characterized as ancient, magical, Masonic, and modern. The most significant survival of the ancient phase is the fragment that evolved into the Bornless One rite. The magical phase is based largely in the system of Angelic Magic performed by Egyptian holy man Abramelin the Mage and set down by Abraham of Wurtzburg in *The Book of the Sacred Magic of Abramelin the Mage*, published in the 1400s in Europe. The Masonic phase has its roots in various mystical orders like the Order of the Golden Dawn. This tradition drew on the Abramelin material as well as the Bornless One rite, linking the two in the operation that came to be called the Knowledge and Conversation of the Holy Guardian Angel. The final, modern phase was sparked in the 1960s and 1970s by the mass publication of all the previously mentioned materials, as well as the notes and texts created by people who had performed and developed the rite. (For more on the history of the rite and the Bornless One ritual, see Appendix E.)

When discussing the Knowledge and Conversation of the Holy Guardian Angel, one question always surfaces: Why does it work? After decades of contemplating this question, I have come to several conclusions:

- It works because it is in line with God's plan that you have access to, and a duty to unite with your higher Self, your Guardian Angel.

- *Any* spiritual program (and that is what the operation is) that you follow carefully and diligently with fervor, serious devotion, a strong will, real focus, and constant repetition will work.

- Your inner mind and spirit respond positively to spiritual endeavor, especially if you are committed, prepare well, and believe in the process you are doing.

- Modern psychology and comparative mythology show that the search for Self is common to all people. Jung described the process of discovering and communing with the evolving Self (the Guardian Angel) as individuation and showed that it can be accelerated through therapy, dream analysis, and creative work. The process of the Knowledge and Conversation of the Holy Guardian Angel can thus be seen as analogous to psychotherapy.

Personally, I believe all of these things, but feel they do not completely explain the mystery embodied in this amazing operation, which is as it should be. God does move in mysterious ways and the divine, as many holy men have pointed out, is always within and around us. Possibly this operation is simply a way to wake us up and make us see this truth. In any event, one thing is certain: *It works!*

MY EXPERIENCE WITH THE RITE

In the Spring of 1979, I had just graduated from a college in upstate New York and was seeking to attend graduate school in Washington State. I wanted to pursue a degree in Ancient History. During this time, I lived with my mother in an apartment in the suburbs of New York City. I had been involved in a number of spiritual practices that could be called eclectic. I attempted to meditate every day, used a variety of visualization exercises, experimented with yoga and the chakras, and had become somewhat well-versed in Qabalistic studies and a variety of Western mystical lore. I had encountered the Bornless One rite as well as the Abramelin book and thus the Knowledge and Conversation of the Holy Guardian Angel procedure. I was strongly attracted to the idea of the Guardian Angel and, informally, began work on contacting and forming a relationship with my own. Within a short period of time, this began to take center-stage in my life. I did the Bornless One rite a few times with remarkable results and soon began to develop simple exercises for connecting with my Guardian Angel, some of which are in this book.

I started keeping a journal—an important exercise for anyone who embarks on an individual spiritual quest. What I began to notice on reviewing my old journals was that my Guardian Angel had begun to clearly guide and help me. Information I sought suddenly appeared; questions I had were suddenly answered in amazing and inexplicable ways. People I had never met before told me things I needed to hear and, in several instances, I had clear dreams about specific items that would further my work.

This was my state of mind when I found myself with nothing to do for several months at my mother's home as I awaited admission to graduate school. I had finished my job, so I was at leisure. Suddenly, everything became plain and my Guardian Angel, both in dreams and during meditation, urged me with great insistence to research and do the operation of the Knowledge and Conversation of the Holy Guardian Angel. Although I balked at such a commitment at first, I began to see that I did not have to follow Abramelin's extreme practice to the letter but could adjust it to my needs. I meditated deeply on this, took notes, and discovered a way to do it that would not remove me completely from the world. Yet I began to have grave doubts. I didn't think I could pull it off!

Then, as I was about to let it go, a few things fell into place. First, my mother had an extra room she said I could use if I liked. Thus I had my temple, one of the prerequisites of the operation. Then, all the texts and papers I'd been seeking were delivered to me in an amazing way by a store in New York City called Weiser's! Finally, as I started to discuss the operation seriously with friends who were sympathetic, they too began to be drawn to both the Knowledge and Conversation of the Holy Guardian Angel operation and the Bornless One rite. We did the rite several times together and it unleashed such power that I decided then and there to do the full Knowledge and Conversation operation.

I began by preparing myself for about a month, setting up the temple with an altar, putting a large circle on the floor, filling the space with inspirational art and other items. I also began to assemble the tools and items necessary, with the almost miraculous help of my Guardian Angel. I needed a chalice or ceremonial cup; one that was perfect suddenly appeared for a very low price in a store that never carried such things! And on it went.

I began to feel my way, making substitutions, asking my Guardian Angel about this or that and getting clear answers in the form of inspiration, coincidences, and dreams. I soon came to realize that devotion, repetition, and intent were the keys to the whole thing. Various texts called for specific robes and incense and other items, but my Guardian Angel led me to see that this was all window-dressing. My angel did not care about specifics, but made it clear that some things, like consistency, were key.

I spent many weeks meditating on this whole process and calling upon my angel with various exercises and meditations, some of which I have refined and put in this book. I knew preparation was key, so I invoked my Guardian Angel every day. Soon, I was ready to begin.

On an especially appropriate day, I wrote out a vow: To do the Knowledge and Conversation of the Holy Guardian Angel operation until it succeeded. I had decided to do the process for six months, as Abramelin stated, though I figured the actual rite would be completed in the first three months, as was noted in other texts. I chose to continue the operation for six months to help me transition to a new life in Washington State and to give me enough time after the operation to accept and acclimate to the new state of consciousness, whatever that might be!

I had a set ritual of my own I used to banish or clear the temple. I also decided to use the Bornless One rite as my regular ritual each day. I also took an idea from another text:

> And during this time he shall have composed an invocation suitable, with such wisdom and understanding as may be given him from the Crown .... Moreover, he shall copy his invocation upon a sheet of pure white vellum, with Indian ink, and he shall illuminate it according to his fancy and imagination, that shall be informed by beauty. (Aleister Crowley, The Vision & the Voice, p. 180)

And so I decided that I would prepare, for the first week of the operation, such an invocation and would, according to the procedure, use this invocation four times a day—at sunrise, midday, sunset, and midnight. Sunrise often became "first thing in the morning," but otherwise I kept to this schedule religiously during the entire process.

With great pomp and circumstance, I began the operation and immediately a dozen things tried to stop me! I became ill; I was interrupted often at the wrong time; letters didn't arrive that were supposed to; many problems appeared out of nowhere— it was amazing! My Guardian Angel explained it to me in symbols and in dreams: Every time we seek to change, especially if it is a big change, there is a backlash. On top of that, my ego or Shadow was quite unhappy that I was seeking to transcend it and turn over control of my life to my Higher Self. It began making all sorts of trouble! I thought of the temptations of St. Anthony, realized my problems were minor, decided I could deal with them, and kept on track and on schedule. After a month or so, things died down and the rite began to pick up speed.

Soon I was in an altered state of bliss as I entered the temple, even before I began the rite. With every repetition of my special prayer, I felt closer and closer to my Guardian Angel. Every time I did the Bornless One rite, the room filled with light. I began to see patterns in everything; the way people communicated, the flow of the river through my town, in art, clouds, everything. I became terribly sensitive to others, especially to the pain or sadness they felt. I also began to spend more and more time alone. Reality just became too intense!

By now I could really understand the instruction in Abramelin that aspirants should be alone and secluded when they do the operation. I became something of a hermit! I began to paint for the first time in my life; I did collages and drew endlessly. I felt creative parts of my mind opening up day by day and I read vociferously! I began to write historical articles, edit a magazine, write pages and pages in my journal about everything from movies I'd seen to the meaning of life and death and what karma was all about! I became obsessed with symbols. I chose a symbol for my Guardian Angel when I wrote my prayer. I began to find this symbol in all sorts of places! It was Chinese, it was Incan, and then, amazingly, a friend sent me a supposed photo of a UFO with the same symbol on it!

Everything I did, said, was told, read, or in any way experienced, suddenly became filled with levels of spiritual meaning. TV shows began to speak to me directly! Amazing chains of synchronicities followed me! When I meditated on my Guardian Angel, I saw a vision in my mind of the Guardian Angel as a rose. Later I turned on the TV and the first picture I saw was a rose. Then I took a walk and ran right into . . . a rose bush. When I got home, there was a rose left as a gift from my current girlfriend! It became almost a game. My friends thought I was being silly! My Guardian Angel was everywhere! If I asked a question and turned on the radio, the song playing would invariably answer my question. If I opened a book at random, there would be the perfect answer as well.

This went on for several months. Then suddenly, I went into a deep depression. I felt the amazing energy, light, and power that had filled my temple and my spirit daily suddenly disappear. I was devastated! Had I done something wrong? Should I quit? I did the prayers and rite daily, but even though I mustered as much enthusiasm and desire as possible, I felt as if my efforts were leading off into an abyss. My Guardian Angel seemed absent. The magic I'd been counting on disappeared. I broke up with my girlfriend and lost a dear friend due to an argument that made no sense at all. I felt isolated and bored. I worried about money, my future plans, and just about everything else. My mom and I were not getting along and, finally, I took a job that was silly and demeaning. Life was hell.

I almost stopped the operation. But I persisted for three reasons. First, I'm stubborn. I'd said I was going to finish it, so I was going to finish it! Second, though distant and rather incommunicado at this point, I felt my Guardian Angel was out there rooting for me. I knew this was some sort of test, so I figured I'd keep going. Finally, I reread the Abramelin book and other materials and they emphasized that you should never stop the operation without completing it. I had also forgotten an important point in the traditional Abramelin operation that others had deleted or just left out: As you invoke the Guardian Angel, you must also invoke all the demons and your Shadow and work through them to get to your angel.

Aha! Now it all made sense. What Abramelin had been saying, in modern terms, is that when you invoke your Guardian Angel in such a concentrated and intense operation, you also have to deal with your Shadow or demons as well. In my case, these demons were laziness, anger, envy, impatience, unkindness, loneliness, and boredom. My answer? I kept on and did the operation daily, no matter what.

After about a month of this, it seemed as if the Sun was finally coming out from behind a cloud and the overwhelming depression and negativity I'd felt began to disappear. As I reached the two-and-a-half-month mark, I began to feel the old power and joy returning as I did the operation. Then, something amazing happened. Something wondrous and unexpected: I achieved, without warning, Knowledge and Conversation of the Holy Guardian Angel.

It happened like this. I was in my temple with a friend who was also beginning to invoke his angel. He watched as I did my Guardian Angel prayer at midday. As he watched me, I suddenly froze and my voice trailed off. I was staring into space with a wide-eyed look of amazement on my face. Then, a minute later, I pitched forward and passed out on the floor! My friend helped me to my bed where I suffered vertigo and nausea for hours. By dinnertime, I was able to sit up and then I told my friend what I had seen.

I was doing the prayer as I always did when, suddenly, the whole room became pitch black. I was floating in space, a blackness darker than anything I'd ever seen. It seemed as if I was floating in the darkness forever when, suddenly, I became aware of a small point of light ahead of me. It was so beautiful and powerful that I was transfixed by it and began to cry with joy. The star got bigger and brighter; I realized that it was coming toward me. I yearned for it more than I have ever yearned for anything in my life. It seemed to take years to approach, but when it was nearer, I saw it was a humanlike figure. It was not just blinding white as I'd first thought, but had electric blue lights writhing in it. Eventually—as I said it seemed to take years—the figure floated up to me. It was my Guardian Angel. It was an electric and pulsing human figure made of incandescent white and blue light with sweeping wings and lightninglike hair. Its arms were outstretched on either side. As it came up to me, I felt blasted by its power and energy. It was almost too much to stand. I was crying with joy and I opened my arms to receive the blessing of my angel. Tremendous power, knowledge, and consciousness were beamed into me until I couldn't take any more and I passed out.

It was three days before I felt normal again. I told everyone I was ill. In fact, I was adjusting to the shock of being pulled out of my body, or so it had felt. During those three days, my mind whirled. I felt like a computer that had just downloaded an encyclopedia! I spent those three days filling notebooks and sketchpads with poetry, symbols, ideas, and essays. They poured out of me! It is impossible for me to either describe the sensation or communicate the conversation I received. It is also useless for me to try to explain the knowledge I received or the effect it had on me. This knowledge cannot help others, since no one else will have the same experience. "The form which the Holy Guardian Angel assumes," Israel Regardie tells us, "must differ for each aspirant who proceeds with this particular discipline. No two students will experience identically the mystical event, nor will they perceive the same Form as his Holy Guardian Angel." (*Ceremonial Magic*, p. 73)

I did continue with the operation for another three months or so. I never again had such a concrete and world-shaking vision of my Guardian Angel, but then I didn't need to. From that time on my Guardian Angel was a continual presence in my mind and soul. The "downloaded" information from that experience took months to integrate into my conscious mind. Twenty years later, I think I am still assimilating information I received at that time!

I completed the full six-month program in the spring of 1980, in my new home in Bellingham, Washington. The final month saw me diving into ancient history and writing furiously. Several times my Guardian Angel told me to write and then dictated things to me. Most of these poems or special writings really only make sense to me, but you can see an example of one of them in Appendix C.

As an interesting side note, a week after I completed the Knowledge and Conversation of the Holy Guardian Angel operation, Mt. St. Helens erupted with a bang and the sound shook me awake! It is perhaps not surprising, then, that numerous images of eruptions appear in the poetry I wrote toward the end of the working.

One thing is clear to me: The real operation of Knowledge and Conversation of the Holy Guardian Angel is ongoing and will stay with me until my death. I have, over the years, tried to do small retreats where I could devote myself completely to my Guardian Angel. These have always proven powerful and renewing. I do not fear death; my Guardian Angel has shown me that there is no end or beginning, only the infinite power and love of God. My job, I have been told, is to do my Will with love and, as Buddha said, to "avoid error!"

PERFORMING THE KNOWLEDGE AND CONVERSATION OF THE HOLY GUARDIAN ANGEL RITE

Exercise 21 on page 105 gives a simplified version of exactly how to do the traditional Knowledge and Conversation of the Holy Guardian Angel operation. By traditional, I mean the clear yet still very ceremonial version of the rite as synthesized by mystics in the early 1900s from the Abramelin book and other sources.

In many cases, the specific items are clearly described. I will add to these as necessary, since in today's world, finding, for example, a wand of almond wood is highly unlikely. While this is more or less the same version I used in my operation, I used particular items as I willed. For example, I used a wand of oak because it is the tree with which I identify. Why is using these rather arcane items in this operation important? Because they can help prepare you psychologically and spiritually to step beyond your normal life into a sacred place where your Guardian Angel can manifest. Several items are symbolic of the five elements or senses that you must call upon to focus both consciously and unconsciously on the Guardian Angel: the wand (air-smell), the plate (earth-touch), the oil (water-taste), the lamp (fire-sight), and the prayer or invocation (spirit-sound). Wearing a special robe also helps you step into this new reality. Do you really need all of these items? It is hard to say. If you feel that this sort of ceremonial complexity is not your style, skip down to Exercise 22 on page 111 and try the modern version! I highly recommend that no matter which version you choose, you personalize the items as you Will and as your Guardian Angel directs.

Exercise 21: Traditional Rite of Knowledge and Conversation of the Holy Guardian Angel

You will need a special room or small building to use as your temple. Tradition says that the roof should be white and the floor covered with a carpet of black and white squares with a border of blue and gold.

For practical purposes, it should be private, clean (and kept clean regularly), and filled with inspirational and spiritual art. It should have an altar, facing east, and you should be able to use it without hindrance whenever you want. It needs to be left absolutely undisturbed during the six months you will do this rite. Other items include:

A holy lamp. Tradition says it should be an oil lamp with red glass burning olive oil, should be hung from the ceiling over the altar, and should burn continuously for the length of the operation. For practical purposes, any lamp or large candle will do. I used a big glass-enclosed candle that lasted me for many months and could take refills. I used white, but gold or yellow are also appropriate. I did not leave it burning when I was not in the temple—fire hazard!

An incense burner and holy incense. Tradition says the burner should be a hemisphere made of gold, silver, and copper. The traditional incense is made of olibanum, stacte, and lignum aloe or cedar or sandalwood. For practical purposes, you can burn any incense you feel is sacred or holy, especially if it relates to your Guardian Angel. Everyone is different! I used an incense burner I already had made of brass and I burned frankincense.

A flask of holy oil. Tradition says the oil should be made of myrrh, cinnamon, and galangal and kept in a crystal vial or flask. I actually did use this oil since it was relatively easy to make and was quite powerful. I know others who used rose and jasmine oil or sandalwood. It is up to you. I've never seen a crystal flask! I used a nice glass one. Again, do as your Guardian Angel indicates.

A wand of holy wood. Tradition says the wand should be almond or hazel wood and should be cut from a tree at equinox, solstice, or other holy day. I used an oak wand, as I mentioned, that had been cut from a tree by me on my birthday! Again, make it meaningful for you.

A robe. Tradition says the robe should have all sorts of sacred symbols on it and be made of specific colors (purple, green, blue, gold, and red inside!). For practical purposes, use a simple new robe or special clothing of any type for this rite. A simple robe of white or even a shawl will work. I used a simple green robe because I love green.

A plate with a holy symbol on it. Tradition says the symbol should be the holy square from the Abramelin book or a special mystical device. For practical purposes, the plate should have a symbol on it that represents your Guardian Angel. I painted my symbol on the plate; a friend engraved it. The plate represents Earth and the presence of your Guardian Angel on Earth, so the symbol is absolutely up to you.

A filet (headband). Tradition says you should wear a filet or headband made of laurel, rose, ivy, or rue and then burn it in the censer when each day is done! Fire codes probably forbid burning laurel filets in your home! I had a simple headband I created of cloth with some symbols sacred to me on it. I wore this in the temple.

A special personal prayer. Tradition says you will receive this special prayer from your Guardian Angel during the beginning weeks of the rite and that you must write it on the top of the altar then copy it down onto vellum or paper to read during the rite, repeatedly, for at least one hour. I feel that you should have received the special prayer or invocation from your Guardian Angel *before* you begin the operation, along with a personal Guardian Angel symbol for the plate. To me, receiving these indicated that I was ready to do the operation. I did not write it on the altar (it wasn't my furniture!). I just wrote it by hand in a nice calligraphic style on a beautiful piece of parchment and kept it on the altar. It was *not* read for an hour; it took perhaps five minutes to say!

Holy books. Traditional Abramelin notes say that scripture should be present, whatever that means to you. Other holy books are sometimes mentioned besides the Bible, Koran or Torah—the Tao Te Ching, Buddhist Sutras and other books of the law of God. It's completely up to you.

There are many things you should do before you officially begin your Knowledge and Conversation of the Holy Guardian Angel operation, as you are getting all these items together and altering a room in your home for the work. I recommend that you spend from one to three months in preparation before doing the operation. Some people I know spent a year in preparation. Choose a daily exercise, from this book if you like, and do it daily. Begin to keep a daily record of your thoughts, inspirations, and dreams. Here are some other suggestions for preparing yourself:

Read and study about the Guardian Angel daily. This may mean reading this book, other information online or in the library about the Guardian Angel, or simply reading and studying holy books or books that are spiritually inspired. Poetry is great! Rereading *Man and His Symbols* by Jung was, for me, mind-blowing. Let your Guardian Angel guide you!

Meditate on the Guardian Angel every day. Spend at least twenty minutes a day in meditation, contemplation, or prayer, focusing on the divine and your Guardian Angel. Part of this meditation time should be spent directly visualizing or at least attempting to communicate directly with your Guardian Angel.

Dedicate everything you eat and drink to the divine. This is a very simple act that is full of tremendous power. You need not say grace over everything you eat and drink; a small silent prayer or dedication is enough. The goal is to bring into your body as much positive energy and divine blessing as possible.

Purify yourself physically, mentally, emotionally, and spiritually. This will mean different things to different people. The bottom line is that you should keep yourself and your living area cleaner and better-tended than usual and should do your best to eliminate negative thoughts and feelings from your everyday life through meditation or prayer. It is traditional to purify yourself with daily baths to which salt or the herb hyssop have been added. Do *not* go into the operation with unresolved emotional baggage; it will sabotage the whole process.

Before you begin, decide what rite or prayer you wish to use aside from the special prayer given to you by your Guardian Angel. One tradition recommends the Bornless One rite, a new version of which you will find further on in this chapter. But you don't have to use this rite. Abramelin the Mage says, "I have not wished to give unto you any special form of prayers and orations, so that ye yourselves may learn from and of yourselves how to pray." (*Book of Sacred Magic*, p. 65). It is entirely up to you what you use, but choose something powerful and meaningful to you. Remember, an important part of this rite is praying from the heart with no script or special written prayers. Devotion, dedication, and spiritual ardor are the keys.

When you are ready to begin, make sure your temple is clean and purified. It is traditional to scatter and then sweep up some salt or to in some way banish all negative energies. On the special day you choose to begin, purify yourself, dress in the sacred robe and filet, and enter the temple at dawn. It is best to begin on a Full Moon.

Arrange the items you have gathered on the sacred altar in a pleasing manner along with any other sacred images or symbols that have meaning for you. The plate with the symbol on it should be in the center, as should the prayer given to you by your Guardian Angel.

Consecrate and bless the temple as you like with whatever prayers and invocations you wish. It is traditional to bless the temple with fire and holy water, but it is up to you. You may say a simple prayer such as:

I call down the love of God
To bless and empower this temple!
I call down the will of God
To bless and empower this temple!
I call down the peace, joy, and power of God
To bless and empower this temple!
May this sacred and divine place
Be a center of light, life, liberty, and love
That it may be a pleasing sanctuary
Within which my Guardian Angel will dwell!
By the power of the divine light
So may it be!
The will to love is the law to live!

Anoint yourself and all your items with a little of the holy oil, saying a prayer of blessing that you choose, or simply pray from the heart. Then visualize or cast a circle of white light about your temple and light the candle and incense with another prayer of your choosing.

Do whatever general ritual or prayer you have chosen, whether it is the Bornless One or another. It does not matter as long as you do it with intense devotion and focus. Then, read the special prayer that your Guardian Angel has given you. At this point you should have built up your devotional energy and worked yourself up into a powerful emotional and spiritual state of mind. Utter this prayer with every ounce of power and ardor you can muster. Make it *real* and *intense!* Then let go of the energy. Relax, even sit in a chair or lie on the floor. Pray and meditate on your Guardian Angel for about an hour.

When you are done, say a parting prayer of your choosing. It can be spontaneous and from the heart, or it may look something like this:

**Praise be to God
Praise be to the infinite light of truth and love
Praise be to the will of the divine
Praise be to my Guardian Angel!
May you come into my life
Every hour of every day
Bringing divine love and will
That I may be one with you
Abide with me
As I go forth into the world
That I may do your work!
The will to love is the law to live!**

Finally, put out the incense and candle and leave.

The operation should be timed as follows:

- The first month (a lunar month is counted, in several sources, from Full Moon to Full Moon), do this full rite in your temple once a day, at dawn (or early morning!).

- The second month, do this rite in your temple twice a day, at dawn and at noon.

- The third month, do it three times a day, at dawn, noon, and sunset.

- The fourth, fifth, and sixth months, do this rite in your temple four times a day, at dawn, noon, sunset, and midnight.

Some texts say that you should do this rite seven times a day (the four times mentioned and three more as well) during the last week of the operation. This is up to you.

On the last day of the operation, at the end of six lunar months, plan to spend the entire twenty-four hours in the temple. Some texts recommend fasting; that is up to you. Bring to the temple your journal and pens. Begin the day with the rite as explained, but do not let go and relax. By this time, you should have built up a tremendous store of spiritual energy in both yourself and in the temple. Pray continually and intensely for hours. With all your might, yearn for and desire union with your Guardian Angel! When you can stand it no more, take the special Guardian Angel prayer you have written that sits on your altar and burn it. Let the ashes fall to the plate. Exhaust yourself with such spiritual intensity and prayer and desire for your Guardian Angel that you are close to fainting! Your Holy Guardian Angel will manifest itself. It will happen in different ways for different people. You may receive an actual vision. Write down everything you hear or experience.

Spend the next three days in the temple as much as you can, communing with your Guardian Angel. You may want to sleep there as well, for dreams will be very important at this time. The operation culminates in different ways for different people. But, as Abramelin says: "In one word, you shall be received by him [the Guardian Angel] with such affection that this description I here give unto you shall appear as a mere nothing in comparison" (*Book of the Sacred Magic*, p. 84).

It is very important that you spend a few months after the experience contemplating it and integrating the flood of new knowledge and bliss into your life. It is likely that your Guardian Angel will have had you write a number of things. Go over these and think about them in detail. Relax, you will likely feel a letdown after the rite is over; this is natural. Whatever you do or feel, remain in close contact with your angel. Listen to your inner voice and let your angel offer guidance and help. You will now be tuned into this divine being, but others may think you have become a bit odd!

At some point at the end of the three days of Knowledge and Conversation, you must officially shut down the operation. You may keep the items assembled for the rite or get rid of them. It is traditional to burn or offer to water those ritual items you wish to release. Everything should be done with great care and with prayer as your Guardian Angel instructs you.

In our modern world, where time is such a precious commodity, doing the traditional Knowledge and Conversation of the Holy Guardian Angel rite may be close to impossible for many people. While I was able to begin the operation in the traditional fashion, several months into it such things as work and moving across country began to interfere! I then evolved a more streamlined version of the operation that I used to great effect. It does not require many hours spent in a special temple. As long as your devotion and desire for union with your angel is strong, and as long as you prepare well, this should work for you. Notice that the modern version takes about eleven weeks as opposed to six months! Final note: Each operation assumes the Guardian Angel will appear at the end of the operation. As I found out, it may be sooner!

Exercise 22: Modern Rite of Knowledge and Conversation of the Holy Guardian Angel

Prepare yourself as explained above for the traditional version. Preparation is essential and I recommend even more intensive preparation if you are going to do this abbreviated version.

There is only one important change in the way you prepare yourself: You should practice visualizing an astral or imaginary temple with the altar in it. The altar should resemble one you would set up for the traditional version. Practice this visualization for several weeks until your "inner temple" is easy for you to imagine and keep in focus. Now, if preparing a temple is impossible, set up a small altar in a quiet secluded corner of your living space. I set mine up, after I moved, in my bedroom. When you are not able to actually use this altar for your operation, you will rely on your "inner altar".

All the items you need are essentially the same as described for the traditional rite, with a few exceptions. I stopped using the robe and filet and instead wore a special necklace and ring during the rite. I felt these served the same purpose and they were much easier to wear out and about! Other ritual items should be kept on the small altar you prepare. Make sure your home and altar area are clean and purified before beginning the operation. Scatter and then sweep up some salt or in some way banish all negative energies.

At dawn on the special day you choose to begin, purify yourself, and meditate before your altar. Visualize your inner temple as clearly as you can before you begin.

It is best that you begin on a Full Moon. If you have not already, arrange your ritual items on the sacred altar along with any other images or symbols that have meaning for you. The plate with the symbol on it should be in the center, as should the prayer given to you by your Guardian Angel.

Consecrate and bless your altar and your inner temple as you like with whatever prayers and invocations you wish. It is traditional to bless the temple with fire and holy water, but it is up to you. You may say a simple prayer like the one given for the traditional rite.

Anoint yourself and all your items with a little of the holy oil, saying a prayer of blessing that you choose, or simply pray from the heart. Then, visualize or cast a circle of white light about your temple; light the candle and incense with another prayer of your choosing. Then offer whatever general ritual or prayer you have chosen, the Bornless One or another. It does not matter as long as you do it with intense devotion and focus.

Read the special prayer that your Guardian Angel gave you. By this time, you should have built up your devotional energy and worked yourself up into a powerful emotional and spiritual state of mind. Utter this prayer with every ounce of power and ardor you can. Make it *real* and *intense!* Then, let go of the energy. Relax, even sit in a chair or lie on the floor. Pray and meditate on your Guardian Angel for around an hour.

When done, say a parting prayer of your choosing. It can be spontaneous and from the heart, or it may look something like the ending prayer for the traditional rite. Finally, put out the incense and candle and leave.

The major difference here is that you focus on doing all this in your inner temple in your imagination. This becomes very important later. Because when you are not able to get to your altar to do the rite all day every day, you can use your inner temple.

The operation should be timed as follows:

- Do the actual full rite only at dawn or early morning, before you start your day. Do this every day.

- For ten weeks, at noon, sunset, and midnight, take a break from what ever else you are doing, sit somewhere quietly where you will not be disturbed, and relax. Close your eyes and go to your inner temple. Visualize it clearly. Surround yourself with white light and silently pray as you like. Then, do the special prayer that was given to you by your Guardian Angel, the one that sits upon the altar. You should have it memorized. You may do this prayer silently. The part that may be difficult is calling forth the power, devotion, and intensity needed to make this effective, but with practice you will be able to do this well without scaring your coworkers or loved ones! The key is practice and good mental concentration.

- During the eleventh week, do the same as above. Do the full rite at dawn and the prayer meditation at noon, sunset, and midnight. Also do the simple silent Guardian Angel prayer and meditation/visualization at three other times during the day, at midmorning, afternoon, and twilight. You will thus be doing your Guardian Angel prayer seven times a day.

On the last day of the operation, at the end of eleven weeks, plan to spend the entire twenty-four hours in front of your altar. If this is not possible due to your living situation, go somewhere where you can be undisturbed and set up the altar there. Some texts recommend fasting; that is up to you. Bring your journal and pens.

Begin the day with the full rite you have been doing at dawn. Clearly visualize your inner temple *with your eyes open*. Then, continue to inflame yourself with prayer until you are swept away in the bliss and power and love of your Guardian Angel, but do not let go and relax. You may repeat your special Guardian Angel prayer over and over, as well as praying from your heart. By this time, you should have built up a tremendous store of spiritual energy in both yourself and in your inner temple. Pray continually and intensely for hours. With all your might, yearn and desire union with your Guardian Angel! When you can stand it no more, take the special Guardian Angel prayer you have written and burn it. Let the ashes fall to the plate. Exhaust yourself with such religious intensity and prayer and desire for your Guardian Angel that you are close to fainting! Your Holy Guardian Angel will manifest itself.

This will happen in different ways for different people. You may receive a vision, or hear a voice. Write down everything you hear or experience. If you can, take the next three days off from school or work. Spend these three days in front of your altar as much as you can, communing with your Guardian Angel. You may want to sleep there as well, for dreams will be very important at this time.

It is very important that you spend a few months after the experience contemplating it and integrating the flood of new knowledge and bliss into your life. Whatever you do or feel, remain in close contact with your angel. Listen to your inner voice and let your angel offer guidance and help. You will now be tuned into this divine being, but others may think you have become a bit odd!

At some point at the end of the three days, you must officially shut down the operation. You may keep the items assembled for this rite or get rid of them. It is traditional to burn or offer to water those ritual items you wish to release. Everything should be done with great care and with prayer as your Guardian Angel instructs you.

THE BORNLESS ONE RITUAL

The Bornless One rite, a newly compiled version of which follows, has a long and interesting history that essentially parallels that of the Knowledge and Conversation of the Holy Guardian Angel operation. It is important to make clear that, although this ritual and the operation have different origins, since the early 1900s the two have become entwined and are often discussed and used together. Over the years, the method of the Knowledge and Conversation operation as set out in Abramelin was extracted and refined and the rite of the Bornless One was used as the centerpiece for that method.

It is also important to note that you need not use the Bornless One invocation when you do the Knowledge and Conversation operation. It may not appeal to you; it may seem silly; it may even seem to contradict your own religious teachings. Abraham of Wurtzburg, who wrote the Abramelin book, was a devout Jew, as was Abramelin the Mage. In the book, he mentions use of the Psalms repeatedly and tells the reader to pray from the heart with devotion.

The Bornless One rite was first printed by Charles Goodwin, a member of the Cambridge Antiquarian Society, in 1852 in a monograph entitled *A Fragment of a Graeco-Egyptian Ritual* that gave the Greek text with accompanying translation and notes. The rite itself dates from around 100 B.C.–300 A.D., but clearly contains words of power that are of Egyptian, Greek, and Hebrew origin.

In the modern era, the Bornless One rite has been reworked, changed, renewed, and revised many times. Recently scholars have been returning to the original text, which has been reprinted and translated in recent books like *The Greek Magical Papyri in Translation*, edited by Hans Dieter Betz. The following revision of the Bornless One rite, for which I thank the scholar and historian Shade Oroboros, is new, but is based on all the existing versions of this text. (For more information on this version, see Appendix D.) It is presented here for your use within the Knowledge and Conversation operation. It has proven very effective for me and for many others.

Exercise 23: The Bornless One Rite

AOTH ABRAOTH BASYM ISAK SABAOTH IAO!
Thee I summon and invoke,
Thee, the Bornless One!
Thee, who created the Earth and heaven,
Thee, who created the night and day,
Thee, who created the darkness and light!
Thou art Asar-un-nefer, thou art Rahorakty,
    whom none hath ever seen!
Thou art Ia-Bez, thou art Ia-Apophis!
Thou hast distinguished between the just and the unjust,

thou hast made the female and the male,
thou hast formed the seed and the fruit,
thou hast made men to love one another,
and to hate one another.

I am [name] thy prophet,
unto whom thou hast revealed thy mysteries, the ceremonies of
Khem.
Thou hast produced the moist and the dry, and all manner of life.
Hear me! I am the messenger of Ptah-Amoun-Ra;
I will speak thy true name, handed down to the prophets of AL.

Hear me!

ARBATHIAO REIBET ATHELEBERSETH ARA BLATHA ALBEU EBENPHICHI CHITASGOE IBAOTH IAO

Hear me, and make all spirits subject unto me, so that every spirit of the firmament and of the aethyr, upon the Earth and under the Earth, on dry land and in the water, of whirling air and of rushing fire, and every spell and scourge of God may be obedient unto me!

I call upon thee, the terrible and invisible god,
dwelling in the empty wind, the void place of the spirit!

AROGOGOROBRAO SOCHOU MODORIO PHALARCHAO OOO AEPE

Holy and bornless one!

Hear me, and make all spirits subject unto me, so that every spirit of the firmament and of the aethyr, upon the Earth and under the Earth, on dry land and in the water, of whirling air and of rushing fire, and every spell and scourge of God may be obedient unto me!

Hear me!

ROUBRIAO MARI ODAM BAABNABAOTH ASSS ADONAI APH-NIAO ITHOLETH ABRASAX AEOOI ISCHURE

Mighty and bornless one!

Hear me, and make all spirits subject unto me, so that every spirit of the firmament and of the aethyr, upon the Earth and under the Earth, on dry land and in the water, of whirling air and of rushing fire, and every spell and scourge of God may be obedient unto me!

I invoke thee!

MABARRAIO IOEL KOTHA ATHOREBALO ABRAOTH

Hear me, and make all spirits subject unto me, so that every spirit of the firmament and of the aethyr, upon the Earth and under the Earth, on dry land and in the water, of whirling air and of rushing fire, and every spell and scourge of God may be subject unto me!

Hear me!

AOTH ABRAOTH BASYM ISAK SABAOTH IAO

This is the lord of the gods,
this is the lord of the universe,
this is he whom the winds fear,
this is he who made all things by the command of his voice,
lord of all things, king, ruler, and healer!

Hear me, and make all spirits subject unto me, so that every spirit of the firmament and of the aethyr, upon the Earth and under the Earth, on dry land and in the water, of whirling air and of rushing fire, and every spell and scourge of God may be obedient unto me!

IEOU PYR IOU PYR IAOT IAEO IOOU ABRASAX SABRIAM OO YY EY OO YY ADONAIE, EDE EDU ANGELOS TON THEON, ANLALA LAI GAIA APA DIACHANNA CHORYN

I am he, the bornless spirit, having sight in the feet;
    the mighty one who speaks the Word of the immortal fire!
I am he, the act of revealing truth!
I am he, who hates that ill-deeds should be done in the world!
I am he, whose name makes the lightning flash
    and the thunder roll!
I am he, whose seed is the shower
    that falls upon the earth that it may teem!
I am he, whose mouth is utterly aflame!
I am he, the begetter and the destroyer and the bringer-forth!
I am he, the Grace of the Aeon!
The heart of the world encircled with a serpent is my name!

Come thou forth and follow me, and make all spirits subject unto me, so that every spirit of the firmament and of the aethyr, upon the Earth and under the Earth, on dry land and in the water, of whirling air and of rushing fire, and every spell and scourge of God the vast one may be obedient unto me!

Great is my might, greater still my might through you!

    IAO! SABAOTH!
Such are the words!

Chapter 9:

Merging with Your Guardian Angel

Once your Guardian Angel is a dynamic and significant part of your life, everything changes, yet nothing changes. Remember the Zen proverb:

Before enlightenment, chopping wood and carrying water.
After enlightenment, chopping wood and carrying water.

What changes completely are your perceptions, your ways of seeing the universe. Values, goals, hobbies, and relationships may also change, but the process of your spiritual transformation is individual and unique and mostly internal. Friends and family will likely see no great changes at first; they will see the same person going to the same job and interacting with the same family. Yet the inner changes in you will be amazing and, eventually, they will transform your outer world.

Coming to terms with this reality shift may take a little doing and certain patterns in your life that were taken for granted may have to be changed. You may alter habits, care more for others, be more creative, or just simply lead a happier, more focused life. Negative attitudes and pessimism will often give way to more positive actions and mindsets. Your Guardian Angel will not make gold appear from the sky or remove all your problems, but it will help you solve the problems you can and increase your ability to generate prosperity and joy. The beauty and power of the infinite life-force will become more apparent in everything and everybody, and its mysteries will become more understandable.

After you have completed the Knowledge and Conversation rite, you will probably feel let down, as after any exciting adventure. This is a time to let the dust settle, as it were, to review the records you kept and to access your relationship with your Guardian Angel now that it has reached a new level if intimacy.

As you come to terms with this new relationship and begin to settle into a more intimate communication with your angel, it will become clear to you that the goal of the Knowledge and Conversation ritual is integration. That is, you will merge with your Guardian Angel more and more, as much as you can on the physical plane of being. As you follow your True Will, you literally become your Guardian Angel.

This chapter is a general guide on how to help make the adjustments required to integrate your Guardian Angel into your being on all different levels of your existence, from the physical to the spiritual. In doing this, you will become closer and closer to the divine in you. Ancient Qabalists referred to one so integrated as "Adam Kadamon," or the perfected man who contains the universe.

In practical terms, this means that your life will be transformed by the clarity and increased awareness your Guardian Angel and you bring to it. You will see mistakes before they happen; you will be able to correct errors of judgment more easily; you will find yourself understanding the dynamics or patterns behind situations more and more. You will logically see where things are headed and know when people are deceiving or controlling you with greater clarity. You will begin to follow your own bliss, seeking both your own personal fulfillment and ways to help those around you. As your communication with your Guardian Angel increases and becomes second nature, you will know the next step to take in all your endeavors, and you will act upon that knowledge.

Knowledge, Will, and Action will become one united process, all woven together by your renewed sense of self-worth and mission in life. You will understand more why you are here and what it is that you are supposed to do to fulfill your True Will, your path that is part of God's plan.

You will judge others less, and perceive and understand them more. You will find yourself filled with compassion for those who suffer and you will not shut out the unpleasantness of the world. You will learn to control your ego and use it like a hunting dog to help you succeed in life, but not to let it control you. Your understanding of your Shadow will help you repel those who would inflict their will or pain on you, but you will not let that Shadow control your life. You may feel more free to enjoy the pleasures of the flesh, but also become keenly aware of their limitations and of the possibility of being ensnared by them. Instead they will return to their rightful place as a sacrament dedicated to further understanding the divine mystery.

You will suffer setbacks as well. No one but the holiest gurus or teachers or saints can keep up the manifestation of divine power continuously! You will seek refuge in ignorance and forgetfulness, let your ego run free sometimes, and slip from being the best sort of person you are capable of being. You are human; it is normal. Yet after completing the ritual, you may never completely fall asleep again. You and your Guardian Angel are now joined and, though the path will not always be easy, you can never go back to being truly unaware.

Will this process cause problems and upheaval in your life? It is very possible that it will—gradually, one hopes. You may make significant changes in your life that will be both fundamental and important. Friends and relatives may not understand. Some who have been through this process have even been accused of "losing it," although they have never been more clear or more aware in their lives. As you change your lifestyle, eliminate things that have been hindering or misdirecting you, and adopt new habits, hobbies, or jobs, it will be difficult to explain these things to your loved ones. You will likely find yourself answering questions about such things with vague replies like, "It is the right thing for me to do." Or, "I'm supposed to do this, I can't explain why."

The fact is that, with the steadying hand of your Guardian Angel upon your shoulder, you will indeed know what you are doing because you will have available to you a consciousness and awareness that encompasses levels of perception far beyond those granted to humans. You have immediate access to your own divine reality check and, if you accept this help, you will find yourself adhering to your True Will more and more easily.

The results will be amazing. You will accomplish more things, be more creative, and be happier and more satisfied with your life than you have ever been before. You will not be able to forget what is and is not important, and you will greet each day as a new miracle full of divine wonders. You will likely laugh more, find joy in small pleasures more often, be kinder and more sensitive, and have a greater sense of mission. In this way, you will also work harder at the things that are important and stop worrying so much about the things you cannot change. You will be more likely to admit mistakes and fix them, less likely to pick a fight or get defensive, and in general be less angry and uptight than you have ever been.

To integrate the tremendous and literally cosmic being of your Guardian Angel into your rather limited and frail material body may be a bit of a challenge. Below you will find specific advice for smoothly aligning the energies of your Guardian Angel with the existing energy centers on your body and the corresponding mental, physical, emotional, and spiritual processes they embody. Exercise 24 on page 133 is designed to help weave the essence of your Guardian Angel into your spiritual being. When things seem to be going too fast in this process or you need some grounding from all the information and energy your Guardian Angel is imparting, use this simple exercise to smooth out the connections and keep things flowing through you.

This will be an ongoing process for the rest of your life. As you gain more awareness, you will also be given more responsibility—responsibility for yourself, for your loved ones, for those about you, for your community, country, and planet. Think of the heroes, the great minds and saints of our times. These are people who were connected with their Guardian Angels and who did great good, whether in a small or a grand way.

Finally, this process often leads to teaching. First, as you evolve and become more aware and more loving, you will become an example or role model for others. You may laugh, but it is likely already happening. Second, one of the characteristics of this process is that those who have gained more awareness must help those who have not. You must meet ignorance with knowledge, anger with understanding, and manifestations of repulsion or intolerance with firm resolve and clarity. You will know what to do, when to do it, and how to do it—never fear!

SEVEN CENTERS OF INTEGRATION

There are seven energy centers on your body, each corresponding to various levels of your reality. By thinking about and concentrating upon each of these energy centers and how it relates to the integration of the body of light of your Guardian Angel, you can integrate the two with surprising ease. This "seven-level view" is a handy way not just to look at your body and the energies it manifests, but to really examine and integrate all the positive and light-bringing qualities of your angel into every level and aspect of your life.

It is important that you not confuse the seven energy centers with actual places on your body, but focus on them more as aspects of your life that extend from you and interpenetrate your reality. Your heart center, for example, is located in your chest, yet the love your Guardian Angel infuses into your life Will, of course, affect everything you do, say, and feel in your reality. The traditional explanation of the heart center as the source of love, devotion, and compassion is symbolic and helps you focus on these things, but clearly it is your mind and whole being that originates and nurtures these important emotions!

How you use this information is up to you, but here is a recommendation. If you wish to further integrate yourself with your Guardian Angel, simply relax and meditate on each of these centers in your body and become aware of how you are changing as you become your Guardian Angel. Everyone is different, so you are likely to find certain levels of reality presenting more issues and challenges than others. If, for example, you are still struggling with anger issues, now with the help of your angel, you will want to concentrate your focus and your will on the opportunities presented by your heart center and what it represents. Often simply focusing on this center and the ideas it embodies and calling upon your Guardian Angel will bring great and positive shifts. The seven centers also provide, in many different ways, excellent opportunities to heal yourself or others.

Simple prayers are offered at the beginning of the discussion for each center or level to indicate the appropriate focus for your Guardian Angel. Use these, or better yet original words like them, to concentrate and work on each particular aspect of each center or level as you need to. Exercise 24 on page 133 will help you focus on all seven centers. Use it to further your union with your Guardian Angel at any time. Again, whenever possible, use your own words, prayers or charts.

Remember, no matter what information is presented in this book or elsewhere, the ultimate authority on living and merging with your Guardian Angel *is* your Guardian Angel. As you work with your angel, it will supply you with exactly the teachers, tools, and help you need to do your Will. Your job is to be aware and to gain knowledge, understand your Will in a given situation, and then act appropriately. With love, of course!

We will begin at the lowest vibration or lowest level of being, the earth center. Then we will move up the body to the highest vibration center or level, the center that is associated with God and divine essence sometimes called OM, the crown center.

BASE CENTER

Traditional name: Muldahara Chakra
Traditional attributes: This center is all about being grounded or "earthed." It relates to physical needs of the flesh, biological functions and physical pains and comforts.

Physical location: The perineum or pelvic plexus (base of spine)
Traditional element: Earth

> Guardian Angel
> You are one with my physical body
> May I be centered in my love of the divine
> May my body be a temple worthy of the divine
> May everything I eat, drink, or partake of
> Be filled with divine love and will
> May the physical world about me
> Reflect your divine love
> Teach me and help me
> That I may become one with you.

Your body is the temple of your spirit and your flesh is the mode by which your Guardian Angel manifests in the physical world. If it is your Will to be an athlete, but your physical body is out of shape, then your body becomes a hindrance. It is through your senses and the actions of your body that you may act to accomplish your Will in this life, no matter what your physical challenges. The genetic code that created you is sacred and is a manifestation of your Guardian Angel and thus of God. You are responsible for tending to this body, keeping it safe, healing it, and not abusing it. This is a sacred trust, for your body is an extension of the divine in the material world.

Ignoring and abusing your body is ignoring and abusing God. The unity of body and spirit cannot be overstated. What you put into your body, how you treat it and the way you maintain it, all affect your mental, emotional, and spiritual wellbeing. This in turn affects your ability to communicate and become one with your Guardian Angel.

Your angel is made of the finest spiritual vibration and light; it simply has trouble inhabiting or effectively coexisting with a run-down or toxic body. Just as you would never invite an important and respected guest into a home that was filthy, shabby, and unkempt, you should think about the state of your body and the effect it may have on your ability to summon your Guardian Angel.

This means, simply enough, that you need to take care of your physical self as best you can. Keep yourself clean, exercise, maintain the health of your body, and be aware of what you put into it and how it affects you. Simple things like food additives, common drugs like caffeine and nicotine, and excessive amounts of refined sugar not only impact the health of your body, but also directly affect your emotional and mental states and thus your spiritual state of being. Nicotine often tends to induce irritation leading to anger. Outbursts of anger and irritation poison your mental and spiritual outlook and this impedes contact and connection with your Guardian Angel, since anger is an emotion that repels it.

Everything in the cosmos, all matter and energy, is connected, and it all starts with your physical body. This center is the base of your energetic and spiritual being. If you try to build a spiritual discipline or activity upon a flawed base, you will probably fail.

Your body as a whole is your "animal self" personified. As such, it has a will of its own that is determined for the most part by genetic imperatives locked into your DNA code. This means that your body responds to unconscious urges and programs that run independently from your conscious mind. Where these conflict with your will, you have the Shadow. Natural instincts form the basis for these urges—instincts to fight or flee, instincts to breed and care for the young, territorial instincts that lead to fights and "mammalian politics," as primate researchers call them. All of these things are hot-wired into the lower aspects or animal parts of your brain and nervous system. They exist for a reason, to keep the individual and the species alive and functioning, but they must be clearly balanced and generally superceded by the conscious centers of the brain, under the command of the Guardian Angel. If your ego is left in charge, it will seamlessly merge with the instinctual, because your ego has a tendency to excuse excesses of the animal nature when pleasure or power is involved.

Your Guardian Angel *is* your physical body in the ultimate sense, since it is you in all ways—the highest aspect of you. Therefore, listen to your body; don't ignore it. Mortifying or neglecting it is *not* a spiritual act, something Buddha figured out. It goes against the spirit in every way. If you have a poor attitude toward your body, your entire self will suffer. Learn to love your body and your Self. To feel good is to feel good about your body and yourself as a human being. This is an important step in merging with your Guardian Angel.

If you need to change physical habits that are negative or heal your body, ask your Guardian Angel for concrete advice . . . then follow it! My angel bugged me for a year to exercise. Finally the opportunity was dropped in my lap and I took up the challenge and did it. This allowed me to move on in my quest for union with my Guardian Angel. I honestly would not be writing this now if I did not exercise regularly; I wouldn't have the energy!

Problems with your physical body can impede union with your Guardian Angel. Listen to your bodily temple, accept and love it, care for it and your angel will be able to use it as a divine throne from which to help you.

GENITAL CENTER

Traditional name: Svadhishthana Chakra
Traditional attributes: This center relates to sexuality in all its aspects, procreation, and fantasies/dreams.
Physical location: genitals
Traditional element: Water

Guardian Angel
You are manifested through my sexual being

May my sexuality emanate love of the divine
May all acts of supreme pleasure always be sacred
May every expression of romantic and erotic love
Be filled with divine love and will
May my internal world of dreams and fantasies
Reflect your divine love
Teach me and help me
That I may become one with you.

This center is the level of sexuality, as well as the level of dreams and fantasies. Sex is a divine blessing, a gift of God, and it should be seen as both pleasurable and sacred. In my opinion, all forms of sexuality are sacred and holy since they would not exist if it were not for God. The challenges of sexuality are threefold and may affect your union with your Guardian Angel.

You must first accept your sexuality as natural, fun, and a powerful spiritual tool. This assumes, of course that all expressions of your sexuality are consensual and do not harm another. All nonharmful consensual sex is sacred. All such sexuality is of God, or it would not be.

If you are uncomfortable with sex in general and with your sexuality in particular, then you are creating a block to union with your Guardian Angel that is most difficult to penetrate and that is, it seems, incomprehensible to your Guardian Angel. Your angel is a complete and cosmic expression of you as a divine being, not someone else's idea of you. This includes your sexuality. If you are embarrassed by sex and your sexuality, then you are embarrassed by God. How absurd! If you suppress your sexuality, one of the most powerful energetic forces available to you, you will generate perversion and negative energy. This negative energy will come out of your restricted psyche, one way or another, as negative behaviors.

Because Western culture has trouble dealing with sexuality in general, this subject may take some deep meditation. You must find a way to accept your sexuality and the idea of sex in general. Listen to your Guardian Angel! It can help you penetrate the sometimes complex issues surrounding your sexuality! Sexual practices, as long as they do not physically or emotionally harm another, are acceptable sacraments.

Sex must be seen as holy, as a sacrament and as a process that exists to continue the species on the physical level and as a way to become closer to the divine on a spiritual level. Guardian Angel sex is the best sort of sex because, on one level, your Guardian Angel is making love with the Guardian Angel of your partner. The sharing is not just physical, it is also spiritual, and this is the mystery of sex! By focusing the Will with love via sexuality, you can literally accomplish miracles. Sexual energy can be used to heal people, to attain goals, and to remove energetic blockages. It can also be used to enhance visionary or spiritual experiences.

Sex is one of the most effective ways to further union with your Guardian Angel! By simply visualizing your partner as your Guardian Angel and having your partner do the same, you will transcend the flesh and call to your angel on a primal level that transcends conscious and unconscious thought. Remember, however, the Shadow also loves sex because it is a vast source of energy that can be channeled in a positive or negative manner. Repressing your sexual urge, linking it to violence or domination, labeling it "dirty" or "forbidden," and thinking of it as something evil or bad, simply channels sexual energy into your Shadow or dark side, building it up and giving it more and more power over you.

Focusing on sex as a holy, wonderful, loving, spiritual thing focuses all that energy on your higher self and channels it through your Guardian Angel. *You* decide with every orgasm. Remember, God gave you free will. You get to make a choice as to how to deal with and channel your sexuality. One thing is certain: Your sexuality will not disappear; it will not be pushed into a box or ignored. Your Guardian Angel prefers that you deal with all aspects of yourself with love and will in the light of awareness and joy, not in the shadow of fear and ignorance. Do this and you will further your union with your angel!

Sex is simply not such a serious subject that it should become obsessive! Sex is a joy, it is fun, it is a pleasure given to you by the divine and you should be grateful for it, not guilty and ashamed. Don't believe me? Ask God! Ask your Guardian Angel! Many different traditions ban, restrict, or vilify sex. But why would God create something so wonderful and so pleasurable only to deny you enjoyment of it! Sex *is* spiritual. Accept this—accept the joy it can bring you—and you will be furthering your union with your Guardian Angel.

Navel Center

Traditional name: Manipura Chakra
Traditional attributes: This center relates to power, authority, acting on your Will, fame and longevity. It is the "furnace" or cauldron of *chi* and bioelectrical energy.
Physical location: solar plexus
Traditional element: Fire

Guardian Angel
You are one with my energetic body
May I be filled with the divine fire of consciousness
May my power and energy reflect the will of the divine
May all my actions and energies be directed by awareness
And filled with divine love and will
May the energetic world of forces swirling about me
Reflect your divine love
Teach me and help me
That I may become one with you.

The navel center is the sphere of the biological energy of the body—what some people call the *etheric* body as pictured in auras in Kirlian photography. In Chinese traditions, this is the center of *chi*, the energy that flows through your nervous system and beyond it. In this sense, it is the center of magical power or the extending of energy from the physical to affect the world around you.

Your Guardian Angel manifests in this level as power, energy, light, intensity, and the electrical "buzz" that accompanies all spiritual manifestations and miracles. This is the level of faith healing, working miracles, and of charisma or projecting personal energy to do what some have called magick or causing change to occur through the Will. This is the level where your personal power lies; it is the extreme manifestation of your personal power.

When you build up this level, when you stoke this energy and work on amassing personal power, you glow from this center. You have charisma, people notice you, you collect energy, fame, and attention, and you affect others as well. In itself, none of this is negative, unless you are driven by your ego to harmful or wildly selfish ends.

Union with your Guardian Angel will manifest here as an infusion of positive and powerful energy—willpower, if you like. Your Guardian Angel will help you direct your willpower in ways that will benefit you and those around you. It is from this center that you extend force and power, for good or ill. This is the place where you learn lessons about personal power, aggression, manipulation, and the ability to make things happen. The negative side of this center is that you can be overwhelmed with energy and power. Your ego immediately inflates, you tend to feel "hyped up," special, more powerful—and you are right!

So how can you use this extra Guardian Angel power? Some, spurred by ego and territorial instinct, immediately seek to dominate others and gather more power for themselves. The key is to avoid this power-mad attitude and let all power flow *through* you; don't hold on to it or hoard it. If you capture and hold and exploit your new power, it will stagnate and eventually poison you. If you let it flow in an appropriate manner, you will be granted more power and energy. As you learn to channel this energy in a positive and spiritual manner, more power and energy will come to you.

This energy is at the heart of the divine; it is spiritual energy! It is the stuff of which your Guardian Angel is made. As you further union with your angel, you will take on the its energetic characteristics; your aura will become larger and brighter; others will notice an increase in your charisma and presence. Yet, as they say, with great power comes great responsibility! Keep in mind that your increased personal power can heal or harm. Be aware more than ever of how you throw it around and constantly listen to your Guardian Angel!

HEART CENTER

Traditional name: Anahata Chakra

Traditional attributes: This center relates to love, devotion, sharing with others, and compassion.

Physical location: heart/chest
Traditional element: Air

> **Guardian Angel**
> You are one with my heart!
> May I receive and give divine love to all
> May my heart be open and my love worthy of the divine
> May everything I feel, say, and do be compassionate
> And filled with divine love and will
> May the love that is the world about me
> Reflect your divine love
> Teach me and help me
> That I may become one with you.

The heart center is where your Guardian Angel takes root in your being and centers itself. Some even call this the Angelic Center or home to the Guardian Angel, though your angel is, in reality, at home everywhere and in every aspect of your being. In many ways, the work of this level is obvious and clear, yet it is easy to overlook. It is the core teaching of every faith: Love your neighbor, love others, love your enemies, *love!* This is the center that emanates love and extended positive feelings outside of you. As you merge with your Guardian Angel and become closer to it, the work of love will become more important.

To love others, really love them and not just project a pretense of loving, is challenging, especially to your ego, whose chief job is to foster self-centeredness! Yet it is surprisingly easy to open your heart with love and compassion once you get the hang of it. It is actually easier to forgive than hold a grudge, simpler to react with laughter and compassion to a problem than with anger. Negative emotions like anger and hate offer immediate short-term satisfaction because they feed your ego-centered sense of self-importance and superiority, yet as they fade, they leave you feeling empty and diminished. Projecting or offering love, however, generates more love and leaves you with a positive and uplifting feeling.

Your Guardian Angel will gently prompt you to offer love and compassion to others on a daily basis, in very specific ways. Everyone has the capacity to love, though pain may have caused bitterness that shuts down your heart center. Your ego may cry: Why should I love them? They don't love me! Yet your love is never wasted; it returns threefold. The more you give, the more you always get, though often from unexpected sources!

Your Guardian Angel is the *embodiment* of love. As you move forward in your union with your angel, you will be called upon to forgive old hurts, let go of old angers and hates, and to love everyone, even those who cause you pain. This is work, sometimes hard spiritual work, depending on what is buried in your past. Still, you have all the time in the world to work through the challenges that God has presented to you, and your Guardian Angel will help you. Love well, love often, and open your heart. As Gurudev Mahendranath has said: The will to love is the law to live. Truer words were never spoken, except perhaps by the Beatles, to whom we'll give the final word here: All you need is love.

THROAT CENTER

Traditional name: Vishuddha Chakra
Traditional attributes: This center relates to real knowledge, speech, and the realization of your Will.
Physical location: throat
Traditional element: Spirit

> Guardian Angel
> You are manifest in every word
> May everything I say and hear reflect the divine
> May your spirit of truth fill every sound I utter
> May everything I communicate
> Be filled with divine love and will
> May the essence of truth hidden in words and images
> Reflect your divine love
> Teach me and help me
> That I may become one with you.

This is the center where speech and words become thought and thought becomes words. Here the work is all about speaking truth, uttering what needs to be said, and not speaking harmful, negative, and unnecessary things. The lesson of this level of consciousness is that speaking must be balanced with silence, that what you do not say is just as important as what you do say—sometimes more. Words are power.

On a spiritual level, your Guardian Angel brings you increased consciousness about your personal power and how every word you utter and every action you do affects the world in some way. It may be a small thing or it may turn out to be a large thing. The point is that, when working in tandem with your Guardian Angel, you become more conscious of what you say and how it affects others.

Words can hurt, words can heal, words can change lives and even, in some instances, kill. As you become united with your Guardian Angel, you will learn when to speak and when to be silent. Whether you follow this gentle guidance is up to you, but it will become very clear that everything you say has ramifications and some things can come back to haunt you. Here again there may be conflict with your ego, which will urge you to twist things said in ways that will make you look or feel good or in some way get you positive attention. I'm reminded of a friend who uttered gossip about a friend she knew she shouldn't talk about (an internal urging from her Guardian

Angel!) and afterward, the words came around and caused the breakup of her relationship. It is easy to avoid responsibility for such situations, but the fact is, words have tremendous power.

In ancient times, it was believed that the word *was* the thing. There was a belief that if you knew the true name of something, you had control over that person or thing. Many religious traditions speak of God (or gods) as naming each thing as it was created. Knowing these names gave you access to the moment that those things were created, a powerful magic. Shamans believed that by knowing the true name of deer, they were able to call the deer to the hunters and thus provide food for the tribe. Stories abound about "words of power" in fairy tales, myths, and legends. There is a basis of truth to these tales: Words *do* change reality. Abrahadabra!

On a spiritual level, all words have a divine power. The word of God, sometimes called the *logos*, was said to have created the universe. Naming ceremonies for children are vital and very powerful in every culture and tradition and people often take a new name when converting to a religion or joining a special spiritual group.

How does this relate to the growing bond between you and your Guardian Angel? As you perceive and manifest the divine through union with your angel, every word you utter becomes important. Your very name glows with force. As you gain in personal power, so do your words. Words are the place where the unlimited power of the mind meets reality; they are a manifestation of your spirit in the world via sound. As you become closer to your Guardian Angel, you will begin to question what you say more. You will listen for interior prompts that tell you to be silent or that warn you about something that is about to come out of your mouth! The most important thing is to avoid lying—not for moral or ethical reasons, although these are important, but for yourself! Every lie is a twisting of your reality and a boost to your ego. I have seen people literally push their Guardian Angels away by lying—they simply couldn't or wouldn't stop. The first step to spiritual growth is always truth. If you constantly invoke lies, you call upon the Shadow with each word of untruth. Our culture is awash in lies and deceit. It constantly bends the truth and submits you to a constant media barrage of selfishness. This makes the work of this level very difficult. To accomplish it requires constant watchfulness.

The work of this level can be summed up as thinking deeply before speaking, understanding the magical power of words, speaking truth, and *not* speaking when you have nothing to say! In all these things your Guardian Angel will be gently guiding and teaching you and usually getting in the last word! Three things will help you with this work.

First, you will gain a growing awareness that uttering lies or nonsense directly impacts your life in a negative way. Your Guardian Angel will clearly show you this happening. For example, your lies or half-truths may be discovered on a regular basis. You will begin to recognize when another is lying to you and you will have less and less tolerance for gossip, back-stabbing, and worthless, empty conversations. I am amazed how many people who achieve close union with their Guardian Angels suddenly stop watching TV or severely cut down on it. Listening to and speaking junk will become less acceptable to you!

Next, you will begin, with the help of your Guardian Angel, to see clearly how truly powerful and magical your words are. A simple compliment may come around and suddenly become a great blessing! I got a job that I really needed not long ago because of some things I had said to a third party months earlier! You will begin to limit your negative comments and begin to offer more and more positive comments, because it makes you feel better and immediately draws positive energies and blessings to you. You will find that you have the power to stop fights, heal people's damaged feelings, make a workplace or home feel better, just with words! You will more consciously control your tone of voice, pacing, intonation, and the way you say things. The Magician in the tarot deck represents words of power; this will be you.

The third and last thing that will help you is silence. You will begin to appreciate silence and your Guardian Angel will show you what a powerful tool for focusing on spirit it is. People often chatter away to fill up the silence because they are afraid of self-reflection. Having bonded with your Guardian Angel, you will no longer fear your innermost self because your angel *is* your best and innermost self. To be silent is to turn inward and to turn inward, once you have reached this stage, is to immediately commune with your Guardian Angel. So, when your angel gently urges you to shut up, be quiet and you will become open to the world.

Brow Center

Traditional name: Ajna Chakra or Third Eye
Traditional attributes: This center relates to awareness and consciousness, self-realization, and enlightenment. It is very much the home of the Guardian Angel and is the focal point of all spiritual exercises.
Physical location: Forehead ("third eye")
Traditional element: All elements united—The One.

> Guardian Angel
> You are one with my mind
> May my every thought be focused on my love of the divine
> May my mind and awareness be filled with divine light
> May everything I think, imagine, and contemplate
> Be filled with divine love and will
> May my inner world be always centered on you
> And reflect your divine love
> Teach me and help me
> That I may become one with you.

The zone of concentrated mind is the key to everything you do and say. It is the place where all things perceived originate, and thus it is the fulcrum or focus point for your Guardian Angel. This is why the mystical or Third Eye is and has been a symbol of

God and specifically of the Guardian Angel for many centuries. In this level of awareness all other levels of consciousness become apparent. The illusion of all phenomena is pierced by inner sight. Your Guardian Angel will begin and end all teachings from this center. You will do your most profound spiritual work here and effect the most significant changes in the way you think and the way you live.

This is the level of concentration. The oft-repeated scientific fact that you only use 10 percent of your mind will become a starting point for your efforts here to use much more of it. Every time you meditate, your Guardian Angel will take you a little farther and a little deeper into the labyrinth of your mind. Every time you visualize something, your inner sight will reveal more clearly how this affects your mood, your feelings, your mental, physical, and spiritual self! As you begin to expand your relationship with your angel, it will lead you to different spiritual mind-expansion exercises that increase your awareness and your personal power and insight, thus leading you to do your will with love in a more consistent manner. It all begins and ends in your mind's eye—the place where you and your Guardian Angel meet.

Your Guardian Angel is pure spirit, thus to manifest it in the physical world takes tremendous energy. Because you are both spirit and matter, you can reach upward as your angel reaches downward. You will meet here, at the Third Eye, the focal point of your inner mind.

Close your eyes. Call upon your Guardian Angel right now. What do you see? You see an aspect of your Guardian Angel that is appropriate for this moment, created by your mind. Is it real? It is as real as anything you have ever perceived with your senses working in conjunction with your mind—which is everything! Where are you? In the focal point of your mind, the place that stores your most powerful tool: your imagination.

One of the most significant lessons of this book is that the first step to doing anything, especially anything of significance, begins with imagination, with *vision*. Great scientific breakthroughs like the decoding of DNA, the theory of relativity, and the discovery of penicillin, all came to individuals who were keenly focused on the mental sphere. They received visions or leaps of consciousness that were not rational yet were very real. This constitutes the chief importance of this level: It is the place where the conscious and unconscious mind meet. The work you have done until now has manifested and placed your Guardian Angel at the nexus point of these two states, what was once called the "throne of the soul." Here, your angel can weave dreams and reality, thoughts and symbols, into visions of truth. You may not emerge from your inner mind with a cure for cancer, but you *will* have a vision of the next step of your True Will. You will "see" important spiritual truths and teachings that will propel you to the next level of awareness in small mental explosions or breakthroughs.

This is why I often advise people to "sleep on" a problem, because your purely conscious mind is the realm of your ego, which may block or trick your mind. How often have you found the answer to a complex problem when you were daydreaming or doing something silly or creative that had nothing to do with that problem? This is what it is all about. Your Guardian Angel will be able to show you how to do this consciously, on a daily basis, by focusing on the center that is in your mind.

The lessons of this center are to focus your mind, to use all its imaginative abilities to unite with your Guardian Angel, to return again and again to this inner sanctum to work with and understand your angel (and yourself!), and to gain more use of and control over your mind through exercises, mental activities, and spiritual practices. You will become conscious of how your mind affects all other aspects of yourself—mental, physical, and emotional—and learn how to control these effects. If you continue to work with your Guardian Angel in this place "between worlds," you will begin to unite aspects of your conscious and unconscious mind to further spiritual growth and to do good in the world! In short, you will unite the macrocosm and the microcosm—heaven and Earth. This was once called "discovering the Philosopher's Stone."

THE ABSOLUTE (CROWN) CENTER

Traditional name: Sahasrara Chakra (1000-petaled lotus)
Traditional attributes: This center relates to the absolute, or God, sometimes called OM or Tao. This is the point where your soul enters and leaves your body, it is the connection between the realm of your Guardian Angel (heaven) and you. All transcendental experiences and the integration of spirit and matter happen here. This is the place beyond conception.
Physical location: top or crown of head
Traditional element: Beyond all elements

> Guardian Angel
> You are beyond all I can say, feel, or sense
> May I become one with the divine
> May I be granted a glimpse of the divine
> May I reach beyond all to the light behind the light
> And so become divine love and will
> May my yearning for the supreme reality
> Reflect your divine love
> Teach me and help me that I may become one with all.

The crown center, the very top of your head, is traditionally the place where your soul enters when you are born and from which your soul departs when you die. It is the door to beyond and, as such, manifests the way to a level that is not only outside my ability to describe, but beyond all ability to discuss in this very limited physical world. When a holy person enters mystical communion with God (such as Saint Francis of Assisi) or enters what is called a state of Nirvana (like Swami Yogananda or Gurudev Mahendranath), that person is said to have attained this level. Those who have, by accident or intent, left their bodies and experienced "heaven" or "nirvana" have reached this level or center. Whether they are saints or shamans, they all return with one thing in common: They are not able to communicate their experiences in rational or logical terms. Often they use symbols, abstract ideas, myths, and Zen-like stories to lead the listener to some sort of understanding of their experiences, but they can never directly express them. It is beyond words.

This is the level where you experience directly the *real* consciousness and being of your Guardian Angel. This is the state of existence your angel enjoys all the time, for eternity—bliss and union with the divine on a level you cannot usually comprehend, at least while you are alive. This level of consciousness is, in many real ways, your ultimate goal as you unite with your Guardian Angel. As you spiritually advance and become more aware, you may achieve glimpses of this state of being. If you successfully accomplished Knowledge and Conversation, this will be your condition when you receive your vision of your angel.

There is no specific conscious work assigned to this level. If it has a goal, it is to *become* your Guardian Angel, a great soul or holy person, and to live in a state of bliss or union with God. There is no book that can tell you how to do this. Yet we know it is possible and your Guardian Angel is there to show you the way, if it is your will to do so. How? That is not for me to say; there are many paths to the top of the mountain. Yet do not despair! I have achieved such visions and look forward to more. Dozens of people I know, regular people, have achieved this state of being and been granted limited glimpses as well! Follow the advice and guidance of your Guardian Angel, do your True Will with love, continually expand your awareness, and this will lead you up Jacob's Ladder to the crown center, the doorway to heaven.

After that, who can say? Your way is unique, your path of growth and attainment will lead you to ever-more amazing states of consciousness and awareness as long as you are able to continue! Yogis, gurus, saints, and other holy people swear that death can be transcended, that consciousness can be freed of flesh. Will this be your ultimate lesson? Follow your bliss and you will see!

Now that you have some understanding of the seven centers or levels of being and how they relate to you and your Guardian Angel, try Exercise 24. The exercise can take fifteen minutes or several hours, it is completely up to you! It will probably make more sense once you do it a couple of times. The goal of this practice is to *align your energies with those of your Guardian Angel* and to open yourself up to accept the huge amount of love, power, protection, and help your angel has to offer. This simple exercise never fails to energize, refresh, and rejuvenate those who do it. It is important that you not be disturbed during the exercise and that you *finish the exercise completely* by going up and then down your body centers.

Since this is a simple yet powerful rite, you must "earth" or "ground" the energy you call up at the end, lest you leave some of it flying around. After doing the exercise a few times, you will be amazed how easy and effective it becomes. Feel free to add things to it that fit your faith or belief system, or to use it as part of a larger exercise. It is also amazingly effective to do this with small groups of people, though each will get something different out of it, depending on his or her relationship with the Guardian Angels. Have fun!

Exercise 24: Uniting Yourself with Your Angel

Sit or lie down comfortably in a very quiet dark room. You should have a candle or two lit or have the lights turned down very low. Relax your whole body. Breathe deeply for several minutes and let yourself enter a relaxed and meditative state of mind.

Surround yourself with a circle of white light. "See" with your inner eye the white light covering you and filling you with every deep breath until you are completely filled with white light. Pray or call to your Guardian Angel as you feel comfortable. If you have done the Knowledge and Conversation rite, use the special name and image your angel gave you.

When your Guardian Angel comes, whether as an image, a being, or simply a light or special feeling, call it to embrace you. Feel your physical body and the body of light that is your angel merge. Feel the love and energy of your angel wrap about you like gentle wings.

Beginning at your earth center (base of spine/perineum), focus your consciousness and chant a special tone to each center, ending with your crown center. As you do so, feel the energy of your Guardian Angel merge with your body/mind/spirit/life at each of your body centers. For example, at your base center, chant:

OHHHHHHHH...

See your body fill with red light as you become one with your Guardian Angel. At your genital center, chant:

OOOOOOHHH...

See your body fill with orange light as you become one with your Guardian Angel. At your navel center, chant:

AAAHHH...

See your body fill with yellow light as you become one with your Guardian Angel. At your heart center, chant:

AAYYYY...

See your body fill with green light as you become one with your Guardian Angel. At your throat center, chant:

EEEEEE...

See your body filled with blue light as you become one with your Guardian Angel.

At your brow center (your Third Eye), chant:

MMMMM ...

See your body fill with indigo light as you become one with your Guardian Angel. At your crown center, chant:

NNGGG ...

See your body fill with indigo light as you become one with your Guardian Angel.

Now, see all the colors of the rainbow that you have visualized turn into white light. This light is the body of your soul and your Guardian Angel combined. Be with your Guardian Angel for a time. Communicate and accept the love flowing between you; it is the love of God. When you are ready to "come back," simply reverse the order of the chants, but this time bring nothing but white light back down your body as you chant:

NNGGG ... (crown)
MMMMM ... (third eye)
EEEEE ... (throat)
AAYYYY ... (heart)
AAAHHH ... (navel)
OOOOOOHHH ... (genitals)
OHHHHHHHH ... (base of spine)

When you have reached the base center, place your hands on the ground and let any excess energy flow through you into the Earth. Say a short prayer to your Guardian Angel and offer the energy to healing the planet or to anyone you know who needs some extra love and energy. Circle yourself with white light again and then go forth and have a great day!

(A special thanks to Oriyelle Defenestrate for help with this exercise)

And then shall you first be able to put to the test whether you shall have well employed the period of Six Moons, and how well and worthily you shall have labored in the quest of the Wisdom of the Lord; since you shall see your Guardian Angel appear unto you in unequalled beauty; who also will converse with you, and speak in words so full of affection and of goodness, and with such sweetness, that no human tongue could express the same (The Book of the Sacred Magic, p. 84).

Appendix A:

Buddha and the Holy Guardian Angel

Holy Guardian Angel: This is a term employed in Western magic and signifies the spark of God, which is the essence of every man and woman. Knowledge of the Holy Guardian Angel is synonymous with the cosmic consciousness.

——*The Mystica*, an online encyclopedia of the occult (*www.themystica.com*)

The Angel is our self, beyond duality. However, the way to understand this twin aspect is through total being, including our various levels of mind, body and ego, our conscious, subconscious and extra-conscious levels of awareness. The knowing of one's self in totality and honesty brings us face-to-face with the infinite potential within.

——Frater Omen

Buddha nature is the basic consciousness of our inherent potential for compassion, wisdom and serenity. It can be rediscovered through meditation, a process of attaining self-awareness and self-realization.

——Ven. Chung Ok Lee

The kind of body, speech and mind that we pray to obtain is the body, speech and mind of a Buddha. Physical positive actions that can benefit, action of speech that can benefit. And a mind with enough wisdom to truly do that which is beneficial. We wish our body, speech and mind to be inseparable from that of a Buddha. This is our goal.

——L. Hadon

If there is any spiritual place where Eastern and Western mysticism meet, it may be in the concept of a personal experience of an actualized Self as spiritually transcendent "beingness." In the Western mystical tradition, this externalized concept is called the "Holy Guardian Angel" (HGA). In Orthodox or Catholic dogma, the HGA is considered an angel of divine emanation specifically born with each person and whose duty it is to guide and help that person in his or her spiritual quest through life and in death. The HGA is also to accompany its charge to heaven (one hopes.)

In the Western mystical tradition, the HGA takes on a much deeper importance; in fact it has been said a number of times that no practical magickal work can ever be done until the aspirant has attained Knowledge & Conversation of the Holy Guardian Angel. This was traditionally seen as an inner and outer magickal working involving the wholehearted focus of the aspirant upon the divine essence of his or her Self through ritual, meditation, visionary experiences, and a complete focus on detaching from the world by "'inflaming oneself through prayer."

At first glance, this process of spiritual attainment of "oneness" with the Higher Self sounds more like a quest for what Eastern traditions refer to as Atman, or the True Soul. On the surface, this seems contrary to the spirit of the Buddhist quest for Anata or the Void, but in fact we can see that they are the same means to the same ends.

Except for the most severely iconoclastic Buddhist sects, all Buddhists focus their prayers and visualizations on specific idealized images of the Buddha or on a personified aspect of Buddha or a Boddhisattva. In other words, prayers, chants, and meditations focus upon an exteriorized image of the Total Self or Being who is transcendent, the Buddha. While we can intellectually discuss the fact that we are "all Buddhas," just as western mystics say, "We are all bits of God," the fastest way to this union with the infinite is to focus on an external image of the divine and then merge with it. In this process, Western mystical rituals and many Buddhist rituals are identical; a godform or personified divine image is visualized and then the adept merges with it and becomes that deity, taking on the aspects of that deity. In Buddhism, one of the main attributes to becoming Buddha is to accomplish what the Buddha did: attain enlightenment and release from attachment to all images and deities! So the Buddhist tradition tells us that this is a means to an end, that what one is after is freedom, illumination, enlightenment, and release from the illusionary world. In other words, in becoming a Buddha, one no longer has any need for the concept of "Buddha," or of anything else for that matter. Supreme consciousness negates bondage and conceptualization, and thus Nirvana or a state of egoless existence as Void is attained: Enlightenment.

What is not so well known about the Western occult practice of union with the HGA is that this is the exact same result that is hoped for after the process of Knowledge and conversation is accomplished. Adepts who have followed this path describe the attainment of the HGA as "becoming one with god" but then go on to admit that one of the secrets discovered through this process is that the HGA is perceived as a "mask of the ineffable divine" or a "stepping-stone" and not the goal in and of itself! In other words, the idealized HGA, like the idealized Buddha, is a handy or useful fiction, a "vehicle" if you will, that carries us over the rough seas of spiritual evolution (Dharma) and facilitates our complete awareness of All as All, that is, as Void.

This sort of consciousness, of course, can only be discussed in terms of paradox, in both Western occult traditions and in Buddhism. In Qabala, this state of consciousness is of the Supernals and beyond. After becoming one with the HGA (Tipereth), the adept continues upward on the Tree of Life to union with God (Kether.) It is what happens after this that unites the Eastern and Western paths of attainment. The goal in both Buddhism and the Western occult tradition is to get "off the Tree of Life" ("Maya" in Buddhism) completely. Thus either Ain ("Void" in Hebrew) or Anata ("Void" in Sanskrit) is obtained.

So, in both mystical traditions, where are dedicated mystics headed? It is the Void, Ain or Anata.

The nexus or place where the Buddhist and Western gnosis come together for me

personally is in the mantra OM MANI PADME HUM, defined by several Buddhist teachers, including the Dalai Lama, as containing the entire current of Buddhism.

Often loosely (and some say badly) translated as "The Jewel in the Center of the
Lotus," it is actually far more complex and there is more to it than I can write about it here.
Still, briefly, we can see it thus:

OM. Mani / Padme. Hum!

OM. Jewel Within Lotus. Union!

Here the Jewel is the Buddha-nature or HGA, the lotus is the world or the universe or
the human body, or all three. The uniting of the Self and self is illumination or
Enlightenment.

It is worth noting that the images of mandala, lotus, and magickal circle are identical
in this context. The alchemical image of the Sun as a circle with a point in the center is
therefore, in this light, identical with the jewel of realization shimmering in the lotus of
consciousness in Maya.

Hopefully this article raises more questions than it answers, and the subject of OM
MANI PADME HUM could indeed be a book unto itself. Yet it is remarkable how many
Western mystics and magickians use this "most used mantra in the world." I will end this
short essay with a few quotes on the "master Mani mantra" to meditate upon in regards to
the union of the concepts of Buddha and HGA as vehicles for the attainment of release
from samsara. Whatever your path, may all beings attain enlightenment! OM MANI
PADME HUM.

*There is not a single aspect of the eighty-four thousand sections of the Buddha's teachings which is not contained in
Avalokiteshvara's six syllable mantra* "OM MANI PADME HUM," *and as such the qualities of the
"mani" are praised again and again in the Sutras and Tantras.*

—Dilgo Khyentse Rinpoche, Heart Treasure of the Enlightened Ones

Thus the six syllables, OM MANI PADME HUM, *mean that in dependence on the practice of a path which
is an indivisible union of method and wisdom, you can transform your impure body, speech, and mind into the pure
exalted body, speech, and mind of a Buddha. It is said that you should not seek for Buddhahood outside of yourself;
the substances for the achievement of Buddhahood are within.*

—H. H. The Dalai Lama, OM MANI PADME HUM

New Orleans Voodoo
and the Holy Guardian Angel
by Louis Martinie

THE TI BON ANGE
GROS BON ANGE
AND THE
MASTER OF THE HEAD IN
NEW ORLEANS VOODOO

Papa Legba and the Two Angels.

Crick...Crack

Papa Legba woke up feeling like taking a walk. Since there were no doors or gates that needed opening he could take a day off and the morning sun was shining so brightly that it warmed even his old bones. He picked up his cane and off he went...up some roads and down some others until he came to a big hill. Now this was no ordinary hill. The harder Papa climbed, the less far up that hill he seemed to get. The fact was that he kept getting tangled in the high grass.

Papa liked to sit so he sat down to think.

"Every step up this hill puts me right back where I started. Maybe I'll just...Lord, what is that buzzing. Mosquitoes been jumping all over the place. No, that's not a mosquito even though it's got wings. It's a little angel.

Little angel you come to tell me something?"

"Yes." Papa heard a tiny voice over the buzz of the tiny wings.

"So what is it? Tell me quick because I'm fixing to go home. This hill just doesn't want to be climbed and it sounds like a big storm is brewing."

"Being so very small, I can see things that get ignored. That hill you climbing isn't what it seems. That's not grass your walking through. That's hair."

"Speak up and stop that buzzing."

"Bend down."

Papa bent down and the Little Angel bit him right on his ass.

Papa jumped up and ran to the top of the hill with a little buzz following right behind him.

"What did ya do that for? I could have swatted you."

"You're where you wanted to be aren't you?"

"Yea, but I can think of a lot less painful ways to get here."

All of a sudden Papa realized that the "here" where he was on the head of a big angel. This angel was as big as the other angel was small.

"I hope you don't have teeth as sharp as your little brother here," Papa muttered.

The big angel didn't seem to notice him. It just went about its business, which at the moment consisted of taking a nap and snoring loudly. His snoring was so loud that it sounded like a big thunderstorm coming in over the bayous.

Now Papa is an elder and elders are not always the most soft-spoken people around.

"Umm...you are one fat angel. How the Hell did you get so big?" said Papa. "With your big ol' nasty eyes and big ol' nasty nose. I wonder what you eat, I'd like to have some of that."

The big angel gave a yawn. A big, fat hand started to reach up toward an equally fat head. Papa started to lose his balance.

The big angel had an itch to scratch.

Way far away Papa saw something big coming at him. A plump hand was coming out of the sky reaching for the head getting ready for a good scratch.

The hand came down lower.

Papa watched.

The hand came down lower still.

Papa watched a little harder.

"Jump," yelled the little angel, "that hand's not going to stop for you. He doesn't even know you're here."

"Mosquitoes jump. Loa don't go hopping all over the place, you sharp toothed flea. Let me alone."

Then he heard it. An if not ominous, then potentially painful buzzing closing in behind him.

"The big one is gonna scratch his head." Papa hesitated. "What's worse, the teeth or that hand?"

Standing between the teeth and the hand, the earth below looked pretty good.

He jumped, landing cane first, and hit the ground running.

Papa went home and made sure he found some gates and doors that needed opening. He resolved that the next time he wanted to take a walk maybe he would head in another direction.

New Orleans Voodoo recognizes the influence of many spirits that can act as guardians. Three of these spirits are the Gros Bon Ange, the Ti Bon Ange, and the Master of the Head. We believe that all of us have a Gros Bon Ange, a Ti Bon Ange, and a Master of the Head. The story above illustrates aspects and attributes of the Gros and Ti Bon Anges.

Papa Legba opens the door or gate to the Invisible World in Voodoo ceremonies. He is also a trickster and the ruler of chance occurrence. His whimsy in taking a day off puts him in contact with the two angels. The Big Angel (Gros Bon Ange) is a bit too big and impersonal. The Small Angel (Ti bon Ange) is a bit too tiny and personal.

It is in the Master of the Head that a balance is struck. As in many traditions, these three spirits form a trinity in which two come together to give form to the third.

Master of the Head

Gros Bon Ange ⟋   ⟍ Ti Bon Ange

One way the Master of the Head can be understood is as a joining of the Big and Small Angels. Nurture (small influences) and Nature (big influences) conjoin to name the Master of the Head. The Master of the Head in this sense is the joining of the Ti and Gros Bon Anges, the marriage of individual will and universal love, the joining of the personal with the transpersonal. In addition, it is the Master of the Head that most closely conforms to the notion of a Guardian Angel.

In New Orleans Voodoo the head is seen as a primary position of power. Each practitioner of voodoo has a Loa (a Grand Angel of Africa) that is the Master of his or her Head. These loa are in a complex relationship with the individuals for whom they act as Master of the Head. They are, in a sense, a very pure or rarified version of the practitioner's most prominent personal and spiritual traits. To know who the Master of your Head is, is to know who you are in a deep sense. The virtues and faults of this loa highlight your virtues and faults. It is as if the Master of the Head is a kind of high-definition mirror in which you see yourself. Knowing the Master of the Head can help you in everything from finding the right job to pursuing the set of spiritual practices best for your temperament. The Master of the Head guards what you have made of yourself.

The Guardian Angel can protect you to the extent that you create an opening for the protection, to the extent that you make yourself available to the protection. This special loa shares the same essential personal and spiritual qualities with you. This loa cares for and understands you as it cares for and understands itself. To this extent you can open yourself to it guardianship.

"Master" is, at best, a harsh term. It is colored with the historically stark hues of the master/slave relationship. Perhaps "mastery" is a better term than "master" in trying to describe the relationship between the devotee and the loa that presides over his head. This loa is not so much master of the person as the spirit that has a mastery of the particular set of behaviors the person uses to organize his or her life. The person chooses behaviors. The loa does not choose for him or her.

The loa are powerful, sentient beings defined by extreme focus of action. We human beings are possessed of a terrible complexity. The loa are much simpler in their rarified environs. It is not within the realm of Legba to doubt the importance of unexpected occurrences. Legba has a mastery of the unexpected. Mammy Waters could not be cold and uncaring. She is the epitome of the kind mother. Ogun or Annie Christmas could not weaken for they are the strength of iron incarnate. We have much greater latitude in terms of actions and aspirations than the loa. Our field of choice is comparatively immense. The Master of the Head does not impinge upon this field; it highlights and brings into sharp focus important landmarks that exist within the field.

The Master of my Head is a loa known as Blanc Dan-i (White Snake). This is a New Orleans loa who walks with Obatala and is often referred to in the familiar as "Danny Boy" from the popular British song. Blanc Dan-i's aspects include an old albino black man and a white snake. This loa's attributes focus on calmness of spirit, clear thought, patience, and a special favor toward persons with handicaps.

Blanc Dan-i first appeared to me in a vision/dream. He came as a not-very-old albino black man who pulled me under the Waters (a common realm of the loa) and looked straight into my face. It was an immensely startling experience, an experience that had a power and a resonance with my life that confirmed its validity. This kind of personal confirmation is common in New Orleans Voodoo.

The last time Blanc Dan-i came to me was about two months ago. I was worried about our dog. He has a kidney problem and there was a very real possibility that it would put him in a terminal condition. If that had happened, I would tell the vet to end his suffering. I sat at a coffeehouse on Magazine Street with the dog and thought about the situation. I had just been told by a surprised veterinarian that she thought the dog is an odd mix of Tibetan lhasa apso and American beagle. This made the dog half Tibetan, and the Tibetan exiles I have met do not believe in mercy killing. If the dog were an incarnation of a Tibetan, perhaps my decision would not be to his wishes. I didn't know but a decision was necessary.

A white bike stopped before me. The rider looked to be in his late seventies and was wearing blue (blue and white are colors associated with Blanc Dan-i). There was purposeful strangeness to the situation that I associate with the loa.

"What a beautiful dog," he said. "Ah, my dog was so old he was blind in one eye, he got sick, would cry all night, I had to put him to sleep. I loved him so much. I loved him so much and I had to put him to sleep."

His eyes were wet with love and sorrow as the words left his mouth. They spoke eloquently of an all too human frailty and vulnerability. I knew then that I was not alone in my questioning, in my sorrow. What Blanc Dan-i acted to guard was my sense of community, my participation in life's unfolding...sometimes sweet and sometimes bitter.

I thanked Blanc Dan-i. No answers, just paths and decisions. The Guardian Angel guards what is essential and in so doing creates conditions that remove the superfluous. To guard is to protect, to move in ways that insure the continuation of what is close and dear and holy. Blanc Dan-i acted to remove my sense of separation. Before the elder came to me I felt as if I was the only man who had to make such a decision. I knew I was not, but felt as if I were. After the elder's words I felt only compassion for all of us.

Transmission or Inspired Poem from the Holy Guardian Angel

LIBER TETRAGON

0. Cross of life and death
And rose are thee
Red Self upon the thorn filled tree

1. 4 and 4 again
One to bind them
4 winds, 4 flames
4 the All
One to trial them
One must sacrifice
ALL: a rose
      Unto
         The Star-Gate
            N
            U.

2. 4 trees and natures
Cubed is space
Relation defined perspective
In the 5th
Blooming; seeding
Dying
Reawakened by the chant of spring

3. Through the Gate
Of dimensional 4
Spins tri-self
Uni-none, found without.

4. Of each there is one
The giving all necessary
In quartering of flesh
Each returns to its element.

5. A Shell dissolves
In swirling colors
A light is left
HAD-IT.

6. Uttermost beyond
This frame
This cross of suffering
In-carnation carnage
Wading through bones of Aeons
Ever dying.

7. Balancing of self for Self to enter
Adjusts the Wheel; It stops.
Axil flow begins
Watering Hell, burning Heaven
In-divide-ual-ized.

8. A redeemed Magickian is a mighty God.

+ 131 + 4/15/80

By Aion 131 (Aka: Denny Sargent)

Comment on the New Recension of the Rite of the Bornless One by Shade Oroboros

This is the current incarnation of my ongoing attempt to make the Ritual of the Bornless One a deeper experience by examining, and to some extent rewriting, the text based upon its various translations.

This is, in essence, an original reformation of several historical fragments. I have performed this rite many hundreds of times in my life, and believe that it has a powerful and cumulative effect in the unfolding of the True Will.

What I have done here, first of all, is to essentially restore the "barbarous names of invocation" to the most accurate and scholarly transliteration available, that of *The Greek Magical Papyri in Translation*, edited by Hans Dieter Betz (University of Chicago, 1986)—the definitive collection of the body of early spells from which this text is drawn. These often obscure words of power combine various god-names, magical and numerical formulas, and vowel-vibrations whose origins are lost in time.

Other sources consulted include *Ceremonial Magic* by Israel Regardie (Aquarian Press, 1980). Virtually a user's manual for this process, it collects all the various earlier versions, including the original Greek text.

Also helpful was the very useful *Hermetic Magic* by Stephen Edred Flowers (Weiser, 1995), who remarks: "Note that the body of the working is a summoning—but in the course of the summoning the magician is transformed from a summoner to the entity being summoned . . ."

Based on all of these versions and my own personal practice, I have also revised the English elements to a somewhat less florid and Victorian form, although I have been unable to completely avoid the dramatic use of some Thee's and Thou's. The divine names combine different forms from various sources with my own preferred forms. I have taken several creative liberties with these sections, which is rather the point of this exercise.

Throughout the whole of The Bornless One there runs a sonorous refrain:

Hear me, and make all spirits subject unto me, so that every spirit of the firmament and of the aethyr, upon the earth and under the earth, on dry land and in the water, of whirling air and of rushing fire, and every spell and scourge of God may be obedient unto me!

While this work has been a genuine attempt to renew my use of this rite in a form less rote, I have performed it far too many times to successfully change this verse; it has become automatic, and attempting to alter it now would simply be an awkward distraction. For the record, here are two alternate versions:

Subject to me all daimons so that every daimon, whether heavenly or aerial, or earthly or subterranean, or terrestrial or aquatic, might be obedient unto me and every enchantment and scourge which is from God (Betz and Flowers).

Subject to me all daimons, so that they obey me whether they are of the Mind, or the Fates of heaven, or the air, or the earth, or beneath the earth. I am seeing the Absolute and henceforth every spell and scourge will work my will (Webb).

Please keep in mind that "daimon" simply means spirit or spiritual force.

The "names of God," which have been restored to their original place at the opening of the text, were originally, in the ancient Gnostic rite, written on a strip of papyrus which was to be worn as a headband: AOTH ABRAOTH BASYM ISAK SABAOTH IAO!

In the Greek original this consists of 24 letters (the total number of the alphabet) beginning with Alpha and ending with Omega. They must also be intoned to open the invocation proper, although all such names are best vibrated or howled, rather than merely chanted or intoned. Where it says (name), insert your own name. Invoke often!

History of the Knowledge and Conversation of the Holy Guardian Angel and the Bornless One Rite

These rites are found in ancient texts in the Middle East, Egypt, and Greece. The *Egyptian Book of the Dead*, the *Coffin Texts*, and other Egyptian texts give bits and pieces of this process, as do ancient Hebrew sources. The Dead Sea Scrolls and the collected ancient texts in the Nag Hamadi Library also contain clear fragments and references to this procedure in many different ways. These sources are Pagan, Jewish, and Christian, it should be noted. Before 1000 A.D., the early Christian church and especially the early Christian communities were quite serious about the importance of angels and of the Guardian Angel in particular. The Gnostic Gospels as well as various early writings of the church contain much information on the Guardian Angel. The serious student is encouraged to read these and other texts for background information and knowledge.

As the ancient world passed away, the concept of the Guardian Angel and the operation of Knowledge and Conversation of the Holy Guardian Angel in a sense went underground in the established religions. A study of Eastern Orthodox or Catholic liturgy shows many different aspects of the Guardian Angel and, even today, Catholic children are taught to call upon their Guardian Angels for help in times of need. In the Hebrew Qabalistic mystery traditions, the theory and practice of such an operation also continued. Yet serious focus on the Knowledge and Conversation of the Guardian Angel operation was left to mystical branches of religious traditions and flourished in secret societies and mystical brotherhoods.

The first time this operation was really revealed to the public was with the translation and publication of *The Book of the Sacred Magic of Abramelin the Mage* in 1895. This work was reprinted for mass distribution in 1900. It was found by a mystic and historian named MacGregor Mathers in the Bibliothèque de Arsenal in Paris, after which it was translated and printed in England. Suddenly anyone who wished to could read the adventures of Abraham of Wurtzburg as he traveled around the ancient world in search of religious illumination, finally finding it on the shores of the Nile with Abramelin the Mage. From this time on, aspects and information about the operation became commonplace among the mystics of Europe.

MacGregor Mathers belonged, with several other well-known historians, mystics, and Masons such as Edward Bulwer-Lytton and E.A. Wallis Budge, to an organization known as the Golden Dawn, which was dedicated to exploring the spiritual sciences, alchemy, and other arcane subjects. Very quickly the operation of Knowledge & Conversation of the Holy Guardian Angel became a part of their tradition rituals and practices.

The operation was publicized by them and several other members of their organization and thus spread in publications (like *Equinox*) and in articles to the popular press during the early to mid-1900s. One exmember of the Golden Dawn in particular, known as To Mea Thereon, published many different ideas, suggestions, and explanations of the operation after having done it himself. In this way, knowledge of the operation spread to the United States and, eventually, to many other countries.

Since the Abramelin work was reprinted in the 1960s and 1970s, several new generations of seekers have discovered the method and adapted it to their own uses. A simple search on the Internet will find hundreds of examples of individuals practicing the Knowledge & Conversation of the Holy Guardian Angel and writing about it.

A final note should be made of the Tantric-Hindu version of this operation, as set down by Shri Gurudev Dadaji Mahendranath, a Tantric guru who recently passed away in India. In his paper *Londonium Temple Strain*, he explains the process in a very unique manner from an Indian point of view, yet the process is almost exactly the same. He was aware of the Abramelin materials and realized that the operation was very similar to a spiritual process popular in India. Referring to how mystical teaching of the Tantric sects explained the operation, he says:

> The problem of the guardian spirit contact was solved by some of the secret teachings of the Ad-Nath sect into which I was first initiated. These teachings are based on the Yogi or Natha sitting in a meditation seat inside a circle. From the circle he creates or rearranges energy to form a cone... The concept of an individual guardian spirit is not only ancient but accepted in practically all religions... I still think that humans can recover the beautiful and protecting influence of their guardian. But to do this, one must first believe in the existence of the guardian and be prepared to do something towards freeing themselves from the brainwashing and muddy mind conditioning of society and removing completely all the inhibitions and indoctrinations which block the path. The more natural, free, uninhibited you can become the easier the task will be (*Sothis Magazine*).

Other Viewpoints on the Guardian Angel

Following you will find quotes from a diverse group of individuals from different backgrounds, countries, and ages. They have all made significant efforts to connect with their Guardian Angels in a serious and extended manner. I asked each of them five basic questions and what follows are their responses. The richness and diversity of the answers tell more about the uniqueness of the Guardian Angel experience than I could explain in another book! Read them all with an open mind and remember that while everyone has a completely different experience with their Guardian Angel, there are common threads running through them.

The following people have contributed their experiences here. I wish to thank them for their time and effort and for permission to use their words.

Dan Bicknell (DB)

Maggie Ingalls (MI)

Rialian (R)

Oryelle Defenestrate (OD)

Shade Oroboros (SO)

Nemus (NE)

Bruce Fanger (BF)

I. In your opinion, what is the Guardian Angel?

I don't think that you can really define what it actually is, but you can talk about aspects of it. I think a great many people talk about what a Guardian Angel is, but because they aren't seeing it from the same perspective, they seem to be talking about different things.

First, "you" or that thing you claim to be your Self, is a part of the Guardian Angel. Jung talks about the difference between ego and Self: ego as the conscious thing that calls itself "me," and the Self as the totality of our being, much of which is unconscious and even unknowable. For Jung, the goal of individuation was to move the center of our Self from the ego-desires to the Will of the Self. But the Will of the Self is something that we can't ever really know, we can only move toward.

To my mind, this is exactly the same thing that Crowley is talking about when he talks about Knowledge and Conversation with the Holy Guardian Angel. The Guardian

Angel is our Self. Knowledge of our True Will is knowledge of the Will of the Self.

But other people have described this too. Abraham Maslow's idea of a transcendent approaches this concept. Karl Jaspers notes a difference between mundane will and the transcendental or Grand Will, noting that the process of transcendence is aligning ourselves with the Grand Will. Interestingly, Jaspers also defines evil as seeing only the empirical (or Existence) and remaining ignorant of the transcendental (Existenz). So, from this point of view, ignoring the Grand Will and claiming the lesser will to be all that exists is evil. (Note: this definition is amoral; it is entirely possible for the Grand Will to direct us to do something that our mundane views may consider "evil"). And I think this is directly equivalent to "Do what thou Wilt shall be the whole of the Law." So the entire reason for concern about the Guardian Angel is to become aware of the Higher Will and to transcend the will of the ego/conscious self. Doing otherwise is the only evil act that exists.

I don't think that the Guardian Angel is God, rather it is a fragment of God (whatever God is). I don't think that the Guardian Angel is Shankara's witness consciousness, either. I think it is a bit more: the witness consciousness with a Will. God (whatever that is) is completely unknowable/incomprehensible; we can only approach it through our Guardian Angel.

But, if you want to take this a step further, Martin Buber talks about the difference of I-it relationships and I-thou relationships. In I-it relationships, we treat other people as merely things, but in an I-thou relationship, we realize that the other person is a "thou" or consciousness just like we are. For Buber, then, God is the sum total of all of the "thou"s in existence. Our relationship to God *is*> our relationship to all of the other "thou"s (or individuals) in our world. The only way to really interact with the divinity is by loving it. But, if God is the sum total of all of the "thou"s, the only way we can love it, is by loving (*agape*) all of the individual "thou"s in our world.

So: Love (agape) is the law (the way in which you don't do evil, as defined above), love under Will (also, as defined above).

—DB

As a Catholic kid, the Guardian Angel was a young adult in a robe with wings on his back. His invocation was:

Angel of God, my guardian dear,
To whom His love commits me here,
Ever this day be at my side,
To light, to guard, to rule and guide. Amen.

As an adolescent in a convent boarding school, my Guardian Angel was the ever-desired Other, perfection itself, as the essence of Jesus Christ present in a consecrated host displayed in a monstrance in the nuns' adoration chapel. By the doctrine of transubstantiation, the divine presence was literal, not figurative. The host was the substance of Christ under the accidents of bread. Substances manifest as "accidents" such as weight, temperature, texture, taste, scent, appearance—the sensually perceptible qualities of the physical world. Dwelling in the presence induced golden ecstasies, Tiphereth trances.

Today I consider the Guardian Angel as the Big Self, the Atman within that is, the Brahman from which existence arises, the Tao flowing through life.

—MI

A version of the self not necessarily more "wise," but could be seen as a self with more avenues of information coming through. If one believes in multiple interacting realities, it could be seen as a hologram where aspects merge and shift so it is not one being, or even one expression of that being, but a malleable (or is that mutating?) access point to those other selves.

—R

The infinitely mysterious intersection between your brain and your DNA. It is part of both Yourself and yourself, on a DNA level. You (Guardian Angel), each member of a species, draws on the collective memory of the species and tunes in to past members of the species and in turn contributes to the further development of the species. As You are able to communicate to the brain, you (monkey brain), can be aware of the subtle messages.

—BF

I believe The Holy Guardian Angel to be one's future self, guiding one towards it. Since there are an infinite array of future potentials and possibilities according to which choices you make and which path you choose, the question then arises, Which future self? Well the greatest one—the Holy Guardian Angel is your highest potential, your ultimate, divine, fully-realized God-self, and thus angelic-self. It is that part of you that you can be if you make the right choices, following its subtle guidance towards full realization of your inherent potential. Thus it is the medium between you and your True Will, as opposed to lesser desires and distractions which may hinder this realization.

—OD

The Guardian Angel is the symbol and focus of a process of Self-becoming. It is a magickal act in which you begin a quest to unite with an entity outside of yourself, and as part of that quest, you change the way you view the world around you, as events become charged with meaning, as the universe becomes an oracular, intelligent, communicating awareness. Mysticism of whatever religion is ultimately about Union with God by whatever name. Where does an Angel factor into this equation or occasion? The word "Angel" means *Messenger*: this Angel is a ray of light passing between the individual and the cosmos, a guide on the way. We can question whether the experience is inner or external until we realize there is no real difference. Looking at the world's major religions, so many have visions of angels hovering around their beginnings; angels bring revelations. The secret name of your Guardian Angel is the Word that expresses the nature of your being.

—SO

Guardian Angel? My contemplation is not so much focused upon the existence of the Guardian Angel as it is with the nature of the experience that makes the relationship so uniquely personal.

I find it useful to begin the process with a simple declaration that succinctly describes the relationship as I currently understand it. Keep it brief and focused. For example, I might find myself repeating throughout the day the following phrase:

My Guardian Angel is My Spiritual Guide" or "I live for the love of my Angel."

This practice helps to nurture a certain awareness of the Guardian Angel; an awareness that will begin to permeate all aspects of your life's daily pattern, allowing you to learn about your Angel's nature, as your Angel in turn begins to learn the best way to converse with you.

Assemble the 5 things.

Build the temple for your angel upon 4 elements.

Let the Umbra Zonule open the door to the heart

Of your eventual Be-coming.

You will begin to feel an immediate sense of invisible recognition. You will begin to view the familiar patterns of your daily actions through a different set of eyes. You shall recognize the one who is "the holy chosen one" who speaks with a silent voice heard only by you—unique to your life, your experiences, your soul. This is described as the process of gaining Knowledge and Conversation with Your Guardian Angel.

The Working is the most difficult.

The best time is always.

The rewards are greater still.

When the mind surrenders complete control

And a bond of trust has formed

In the grasp of an empty hand

And the window of the Mind fills

With the vision of the shadow-priest

Who lightens the way of He-Ka

As the Khu opens—reveals the House of Khabs.

A kiss between self and angel as

Shu and Tefnut pass between our lips

As He-Ka precedes the word of Hu

A secret name spoken by the same mouth.

This is the mystical marriage

The Magnum Opus—inner alchemy

Of self-love that leads to embrace

And eventual union with your daimon.

It takes both fools and spirit guides to come this far

As far as the salmon of wisdom

It takes vision, clear as the sound of a 7-metal bell.

It takes a voice so light it may only be seen higher than eyesight.

It requires purpose, will, truth, an open heart,

and above all else Love.

A love for eternity that is love known now.

May the hand of your angel be open

Ready to receive your grasp.

May the eyes that greet yours

Look upon you with joy and delight.

This relationship is filled with an endless, mischievous delight; the innocence of Beauty enduring Youth, and all dark senses of humor that stimulate and provoke us toward each other—over and over, again and again.

This relationship is as much the alchemy of the wise, the radiance of that hidden stone that that Bennu call home for 500 years every time the world egg must crack, and the Phoenix arises again at Heliopolis from the temple of the sun.

This relationship has gotten out of hand in order to exceed the limits of normal perception, the limitation of sleep in thought, word, life, and action.

This relationship always needs work.

An alchemy of potentials and solutions.

A stone of precious water

The egg of universal mystery—

And the child that is borne of

Future unions yet to come.

This relationship has One eye

One common heart, One shared centre:

Where love is made like honey

From the gathering of flowers that form a garland

Woven of red roses and white lilies

To place around the One you love

Is truth.

Sun, strength, sight & light, these are for the servants of the star and snake.

As the embrace of your Guardian Angel shall pull you closer to the truth

Of who you really are—

As the rapture and the feast of your marriage

Comes and goes, there is that which remains

Always that your guardian spirit—your daimon

Awaits your barbarous call.

To this end, then the goal becomes immediately realized:

A secret name that is uniquely yours to share alone.

—NE

2. What techniques or exercises have you used to connect with your Guardian Angel?

Frequently I work with the Bornless Ritual and variations thereof. This is what I will use if I am specifically wanting interaction. Also, I work with Jungian dream analysis to try to become aware of the Self.

However, when I first started to work magick, I would only work toward the Guardian Angel in specific rites. I am now seeing almost everything I do as some form of interaction with the Guardian Angel. (Besides, if I am part of the Guardian Angel, how can anything I do not be some form of interaction with it?)

—DB

In the Catholic format, I used invocation through passages from the Song of Songs and Psalms, "The Imitation of Christ" by Thomas a Kempis, "The City of God" and "Confessions" of St. Augustine, and various words of my own crafting. I also embarked on a practice of physical asceticism for a time (fasting, wearing a chain around my waist under my clothes, kneeling on bare wood with outstretched arms in contemplation of the Passion, etc.).

I think it worked through sheer fervor, slicing through the language of the Church to obtain contact with Love and Union.

—MI

I tend to utilize meditation over other techniques. I tend to do a "zone-out" and merge with the central access point and see what information areas pull for me to work with.

—R

. . . being in touch with myself through meditation, tarot to some degree, I Ching to a greater degree. Meditation is stilling the monkey chatter. I Ching and tarot of course do not tell of the past or the future; there is no past; there is no future; there is only NOW—the reading is for that instant.

—BF

My first contacts were not from specific rites, but I subsequently found Nema's mirror rite for contacting the HGA (Holy Guardian Angel) in her Maat Magick book; simple, direct, and effective for consolidating this contact. However, for someone who has not already made contact, a more elaborate rite may be necessary. Also I performed the rite within the context of a three-day fast during which I performed much meditation and magick, so I was already in a trance state.

An individual's HGA is a very personal thing, so I think devising your own personal rite of contact is often more effective than using established formulas, although these may provide powerful frameworks (aided by the weight of tradition and invested belief through history) for personal adaptation and improvisation.

Yoga, invocation, pranayama (breathing exercises), tantric sex, magickal ceremony, fasting, and combinations thereof are techniques I use to induce trance states that make me receptive to HGA communications.

—OD

Invoke often, changing the song you use as your understanding evolves. I use candle flames as a centering point for invocation because dancing fire is to me the living presence of the Light. At all meals I bless the food and charge all drinks as a sacrament. Mirrors and reflections are gateways because the experience of seeing myself as other breaks down the limited conception of who I am. One of the earliest ways I saw the Angel was as my own DNA in female rather than male form; a perfect opposite with which to unite, to celebrate the sacred marriage.

Any sexual act is an invocation of the Angel. Jung's concept of the Anima or Animus that appears in myth or dream seems to me to be a veiling of the personal Angel.

Yogic breathing meditation calms the mind and makes the process accelerate.

In addition to fire and reflections, symbols of the Guardian Angel are the Sun as the center of radiance in our solar system, the Heart as the center of life in a human, the blood as light, the heartbeat as drum rhythm of creation.

Opening to Love is an element of this practice; for years I tried my best to practice a Sufi heart meditation: "Turning one heart to all faces, seeing one face in all hearts."

The context of this process is also important. There are actually still circles of magicians in this world, and I and my friends existed in a whirlwind of wide-ranging study of a number of esoteric traditions, and regularly met for group rituals as well as doing solitary work in our own ways. Most of us were actively invoking our angels, most often with an ancient practice known as the Ritual of the Bornless One. I reached a point where I was singing the strange names it contains like mantras in daily life. As a renewal at one time I did take a magickal oath to achieve Knowledge and Conversation of the Holy Guardian Angel and this oath started a momentum that led to success. I also did a period of sixty formal workings of this rite with ever-increasing intensity and frequency, attempting to earth each in prose.

At the same time some very extreme events were taking place amid the circle of my friends and I think that the momentum that group ritual incites, combined with my own will, led to an all-night session where an enormous amount of the lore I had gathered synthesized itself in a new understanding. I tried to record this as my own holy book, which is a text I still grapple with. A further result of this was a fairly long aftermath of inner silence; the constant babble of inner dialogue actually stopped, and I lived in the world in a very different way for a period of some weeks.

—SO

My personal experience has been that my Guardian Angel attracts the company of like-minded magickians who share a common passion for this work, despite my understanding that you may only undertake this work alone.

Miraculously great things happen when you can gather as one will, one purpose, one mind in a circle with a sacramental potluck and several bottles of sensibly priced wine (optional of course).

Miraculously great things occur when we create assembly, immediatism, celebration, and prayer.

I for one find it difficult to imagine a life that does not know the unique form of embrace and consciousness that only the Guardian Angel bestows.

Long before we knew what we sought

Long before we had words to speak

And tears to shed—the Angel waited patiently for us.

Its eyes of peacock blue

never wavering for an instance from yours.

Its grasp older than the flesh of any single lifetime,

Place, or circumstance.

Long before there was an I, there was You

Who created Us from the waters of greater understanding.

The journey towards the beloved: "the next step"

Alkhemical marriage: no sweeter honeymoon exists.

Death & Dissolution: say your farewell once the Abyss is behind you.

Prescience, preshadows, and an angel who patiently awaits the sight of your face and the vision of how far you travel to this place of rest.

—NE

3. How does your Guardian Angel communicate with you and you with it?

Dreams. Synchronicities. These are the only things that I can specifically point to and say that I think they came from the Guardian Angel. But also, I have sudden flashes of insight or overwhelming feelings of universal agape and knowledge that I am part of a greater whole, and I think that this might be part of my intercourse with my Guardian Angel.

—DB

It would take a false dichotomy to do so. Over time, me and my Angel became one thing. Communication occurs with the Universe at large (through another false dichotomy) by recognizing synchronicities and by forming deliberate desires.

—MI

Pretty much by feels and flows. Very kinesthetic, with a dash of clairsentience of merge…
if this makes sense.

—R

Example: I went once to Chicago looking for an interview for a position which in retro-
spect would have been very wrong for me. There was some radio station doing an advertising blitz, obviously trying to develop some kind of exclusionary in-crowd. Their ad, which
seemed to be posted everywhere, was, "This is not for you." I went back to where I lived
and saw a sign saying, "Welcome to your home." Do I think my Guardian Angel posted
signs in Chicago and Grand Rapids for my benefit? Nope. Do I see this as an example of
communication from my Guardian Angel? Yuppers. Also, war is a good example: a number
of times I would have been killed but for "chance."

—BF

Insight. On a good day, I create a work of art. When I return to it later, I find new meanings in it and realize that my younger self reflects my older self, that time exists only to convey meaning, experience only to confer joy. The same holds true for the arts of others; art
is the immortality of the immortal Spirit that passes through the changing world of the
human body. Mythology, books, painting, music, fashion, cooking, technology, children—
all the ways we imprint ourselves in history—form the tapestry woven by a unity split into
multiplicity for the purpose of play.

　　Imaginative use of codes like the Tarot, Runes, or the *I Ching* help convince one that
the reflecting mirror of reality, what the alchemists called reading the Book of the World,
will never cease to amaze. And on a more immediate level: every living being you meet can
speak with that same voice. If you listen very carefully, truth can come from the most
unlikely sources.

—SO

In different ways at different times. Rarely through direct visions or voices. Often through
channeled writing and drawing and sometimes music. I find any kind of artwork a powerful menstruum for the divine self to manifest through, especially if a trance state is established, preventing the intervention of the psychic censors of the conscious mind.

　　Usually communications are very subtle—feelings and intuitions more than grand
visions or voices—and are often in contradistinction to more apparently "reasonable"
options.

—OD

4. How has your connection with your Guardian Angel changed your life?

The only way it can: by helping to transform my will into Will, by helping me to understand, by giving me insight, by evolving my point of view, by helping expand my awareness,
by loving me. By all of this, it is helping me to grow into more than I am.

—DB

It taught me to be sane in crazy situations with some degree of aplomb and balance, and with the assurance that you're never tested beyond your strength. I've often wondered what it would be like to have a "nervous breakdown," but I've never obtained that data firsthand, despite living constantly in Interesting Times.

—MI

I see life as a magickal mystery tour with the Guardian Angel as the conductor. Don't ask what your You can do for you, ask what you can do for your You. BTW: Many people may find themselves happier asleep, which is no doubt why they sleep.

—BF

I see one of the secrets of this process is that uniting with the Angel in a sense implies becoming that Angel; participating in an awakening, a transformation. Union with the Guardian Angel is working to perfect the self. The world would be a better place if we were all our own angels rather than our devils. Living in this state, everything becomes sacred— music a communion, color a sacrament. One thing I have sought in my life is the peak experience; the moment of vivid intensity which lifts everyday experience out of its limits and charges the instant with genuine meaning. We all go through routines in daily life. Much of what we do is so automatic and unaware that we are virtually asleep. The angel, so to speak, blows the trumpet, which awakens and resurrects us from death into joy, from nightmare into dream.

I suppose what I am trying to say is that I like to think that I have become a better person because I have devoted time to exploring myself, to shining some light into my darkness. I will not claim to be perfect, but I have a pretty good sense of what my strengths and weaknesses are. I know myself better, try my best to do the right thing, maintain compassion for all without losing my rage against injustice. I am more complete.

—SO

It has shown me my True Will. It has established a subtle rapport, which lets me know when I am continuing in the right direction for my personal evolution. It has given me an understanding that I am ultimately the creator of my own destiny, that my "fate" is not really an exterior force but my own angel steering me toward my True Will. The awareness that my primary "guide" is myself in full potential, allows me to claim my divinity as a conscious human who is a God/dess in the becoming.

—OD

5. What direct experiences have you had of your Guardian Angel?

I had a dream of "the twin." I met myself and made love to myself (is that narcissism?) in this dream. I really hesitate to share this because I thought it was a bit strange. However, from what I have read, I have learned that others have had similar dreams and usually dreams of the twin are interpreted as the Guardian Angel or equivalent. But it was also a very mythological dream; almost completely identical to one of the Egyptian creation myths.

Other than this? I'm still waiting. Maybe someday I'll get a received text too and then I'll be able to post commentaries on it. Well, I'm not holding my breath.

Do I expect any more communication? Visions and miracles would be really neat, but numinous dreams are enough. Yes, I'm sure I'll have more.

—DB

It's never appeared to me as a personal figure, but rather as feelings and new comprehensions. If it had a word, it'd be "AHA!" I have had visions of individual entities, and I've heard Astral voices, but not from what I could identify as my Guardian Angel. The Knowledge and Conversation (the Inhabiting and Merging) seemed like two selves sliding together in the same body, while being seen from a third point of view I call the Observer.

—MI

Depends on the aspect mix at the time. Mostly physical overlays or visions of feeling (ok, so I am a little synesthetic on the kinesthetic side of things; abstract feelings are how I interact with things). I interpret these things as being the "Guardian Angel" as they feel of me, but not here. I have not had anything ever come up and say "Hey, I am your Guardian Angel," but my interpretation/understanding of the concept leads me to believe that the interactions with the various other embodiments of the inner current would be considered in the family of what it is considered to be a Guardian Angel.

—R

Woke up this morning and looked at the sunrise. It was lovely, and yes, this morning it was raining. I walked in it and felt the rain against my face.

—BF

Synchronicities, coincidences, flashes of insight, the book or tool or quotation that appears unexpectedly at the perfect time, the word from a friend which makes it all clear, connections made in unexpected ways that let one grasp for a moment the cosmic joke. And of course there are my "transmitted manuscripts." How do I address that here? I've always thought of myself as a writer, appreciated words and books. My talents did not seem to lie in music or other arts beyond the occasional scrawl, or some play with collages.

In the course of the operation using the Ritual of the Bornless One to achieve Knowledge and Conversation of the Holy Guardian Angel, I would have flashes of symbolism, mythic imagery, senses of elemental presences glimpsed out of the corner of the eye. No vast fiery visions or voices in general; just a sort of unfolding understanding that I tried to earth in writing after each rite, which in the best events would flow freely and spontaneously through. Often these pieces do actively bring the same state of consciousness back to me. Also, one remarkable exception to my "no voices" comment: once while dreaming, a loud voice intoned the name of an Angel so loudly that it did indeed wake me from sleep with the conviction that this was the Name. I felt that this was a major result, and I always try to remember and analyze my dreams as best I can, considering them as messages.

—SO

Bibliography

Banzhaf, Hajo. *Tarot & the Journey of the Hero.* York Beach, ME: Red Wheel/Weiser, 2000.

Bonner, John. *Qabalah: A Primer.* London: Skoob Books, 1995.

Carroll, Peter J. *Liber Null & Psychonaut.* York Beach, ME: Samuel Weiser, Inc., 1987.

Cavendish, Richard. *The Tarot.* New York: Crescent Books, 1987.

Cortens, Theolyn. *Working with Angels.* Oxford: Caer Sidi Publications, 1996.

Crowley, Aleister. *The Book of Thoth.* York Beach, ME: Samuel Weiser, Inc., 1974

———. *Magick.* York Beach, ME: Samuel Weiser, Inc., 1994.

———. *777 & Other Qabalistic Writings.* York Beach, ME: Samuel Weiser, Inc., 1997.

———. *The Vision & the Voice.* York Beach, ME: Samuel Weiser, Inc., 1998.

Davidson, Gustav. *A Dictionary of Angels.* New York: The Free Press, 1967.

Feng, Gia-Fu, trans. *Chuang Tsu: Inner Chapters.* New York: Vintage Books, 1974.

Feng, Gia-fu, and Jane English. *Lao Tsu: Tao Te Ching.* New York: Vintage Books, 1972.

Fries, Jan. *Helrunar, A Manual of Rune Magick.* Oxford: Mandrake of Oxford, 1993.

Giles, Cynthia. *Tarot: History, Mystery & Lore.* New York: Simon and Schuster, 1992.

Godwin, David. *Godwin's Cabalistic Encyclopedia.* St Paul: Llewellyn Publications, 1994.

Godwin, Malcolm. *Angels: An Endangered Species.* New York: Simon and Schuster, 1990.

Gonzalez-Whippler, Migene. *A Kabbalah for the Modern World.* St Paul: Llewellyn Publications, 1993.

Guiley, Rosemary Ellen. *Encyclopedia of Angels.* New York: Facts On File, 1996.

———. *The Mystical Tarot.* New York: Signet, 1991.

Jung, Carl G. *Man and His Symbols.* Garden City, NY: Doubleday and Company, 1964.

———. *Memories, Dreams, Reflections.* New York: Vintage Books, 1965.

Lewis, J.R. and E. D. Oliver. *Angels A to Z.* Detroit: Visible Ink, 1996.

Martinie, Louis, and Sally Glassman. *The New Orleans Voodoo Tarot.* Rochester, VT: Destiny Books, 1992.

Mathers, S.L. MacGregor, trans. *The Book of the Sacred Magic of Abramelin the Mage.* Mineola, NY: Dover Publications, 1975.

Meyer, Marvin W., and Richard Smith, eds. *Ancient Christian Magic.* New York: HarperCollins, 1994.

Nema. *Maat Magick.* York Beach, ME: Samuel Weiser, Inc., 1995.

———. *The Way of Mystery: Magick, Mysticism & Self-Transcendence.* St Paul: Llewellyn Publications, 2003.

Newcomb, Jason Augustus. *21st Century Mage.* York Beach, ME: Red Wheel/Weiser, 2002.

Regardie, Israel. *Ceremonial Magic.* Wellingborough, Northamptonshire, England: Aquarian Press, 1969.

————.*A Garden of Pomegranates.* St Paul: Llewellyn Publications, 1971.

Sargent, Denny. *Global Ritualism: Myth and Magic Around the World.* St Paul: Llewellyn Publications, 1994.

————. *The Tao of Birth Days: Using the* I Ching *to Become Who You Were Born to Be.* Boston: Tuttle Press, 2001.

Shearer, Alistair. *Effortless Being: The Yoga Sutras of Patanjali.* London: Wildwood House, 1982.

Sophia. *Fortune Telling with Playing Cards.* St Paul: Llewellyn Publications, 1997.

————. *The Ultimate Guide to Goddess Empowerment.* Kansas City: Andrews McMeel, 2003.

Stevenson, Jay. *The Complete Idiot's Guide to Angels.* New York: Alpha Books, 1999.

Thorsson, Edred. *Runelore.* York Beach, ME: Samuel Weiser, Inc., 1997.

Vollmar, Klaus. *The Enneagram Workbook.* New York: Sterling Publishing Company, Inc., 1998.

Wilson, Peter Lamborn. *Angels.* New York: Thames and Hudson Ltd., 1980.

Wilson, Robert Anton. *Cosmic Trigger.* Berkeley: And/Or Press, 1977.

————. *Prometheus Rising.* Phoenix: Falcon Press, 1983.

Wing, R. L. *The Illustrated I Ching.* Garden City, NY: Dolphin Books/Doubleday & Co., 1982.